BLACK FOREST TRAVEL GUIDE

Your Guide to the Best Trails, Towns, Outdoor Activities, Cultural Delights and Traditions of Southwestern Germany

Zeke C. Xenia

Copyright©2024 Zeke C. Xenia

All Right Reserved

TABLE OF CONTENT

INTRODUCTION

A. WELCOME TO THE BLACK FOREST
B. A BRIEF HISTORY
C. HOW TO USE THIS GUIDE

CHAPTER ONE

PLANNING YOUR TRIP
1.1 WHEN TO VISIT
1.2 BUDGETING FOR YOUR TRIP
1.3 TRAVEL INSURANCE
1.4 PACKING ESSENTIALS

CHAPTER TWO

GETTING THERE AND AROUND
2.1 ARRIVING IN THE BLACK FOREST
2.1.1 By Air
2.1.2 By Train
2.1.3 BY CAR
2.2 NAVIGATING THE REGION
2.2.1 Public Transportation
2.2.2 Car Rentals
2.2.3 Cycling and Hiking

CHAPTER THREE

TOP DESTINATIONS
3.1 FREIBURG IM BREISGAU

3.1.1 City Overview
3.1.2 Must-See Attractions
3.1.3 Dining and Accommodation
3.2 BADEN-BADEN
3.2.1 Thermal Spas
3.2.2 Cultural Sites
3.2.3 Luxury Experiences
3.3 TRIBERG
3.3.1 Waterfalls
3.3.2 Cuckoo Clocks
3.3.3 Local Cuisine
3.4 TITISEE-NEUSTADT
3.4.1 Lake Titisee
3.4.2 Outdoor Activities
3.4.3 Family-Friendly Spots
3.5 OFF THE BEATEN PATH
3.5.1 Hidden Gems
3.5.2 Local Secrets

CHAPTER FOUR

NATURE AND OUTDOOR ACTIVITIES
4.1 HIKING TRAILS
4.1.1 Best Routes
4.1.2 Difficulty Levels
4.2 CYCLING ROUTES
4.2.1 Scenic Paths
4.2.2 BIKE RENTALS
4.3 WINTER SPORTS
4.3.1 Ski Resorts
4.3.2 Snowboarding and Sledding
4.4 ADVENTURE ACTIVITIES
4.4.1 Zip Lining
4.4.2 Paragliding

4.5 Wildlife and Nature Parks

CHAPTER FIVE

CULTURAL EXPERIENCES
5.1 Black Forest Villages
5.1.1 Traditions and Festivals
5.1.2 Architecture and Heritage
5.2 Museums and Galleries
5.2.1 Must-Visit Exhibitions
5.2.2 Local Artists
5.3 Music and Performing Arts
5.3.1 Concerts and Events
5.3.2 Traditional Music
5.4 Local Cuisine and Dining
5.4.1 Regional Dishes
5.4.2 Best Restaurants
5.4.3 Wine Tasting and Breweries

CHAPTER SIX

ACCOMMODATION
6.1 Types of Accommodation
6.1.1 Hotels and Resorts
6.1.2 Bed and Breakfasts
6.1.3 Vacation Rentals
6.2 Top Recommendations
6.2.1 Luxury Stays
6.2.2 Budget-Friendly Options
6.2.3 Unique Places to Stay
6.3 Booking Tips

CHAPTER SEVEN

SHOPPING AND SOUVENIRS
7.1 LOCAL MARKETS
7.1.1 What to Buy
7.1.2 Best Markets to Visit
7.2 SPECIALTY SHOPS
7.2.1 Cuckoo Clocks
7.2.2 Handcrafted Goods
7.3 SHOPPING TIPS

CHAPTER EIGHT

HEALTH AND WELLNESS
8.1 SPA AND WELLNESS RETREATS
8.1.1 Top Spas
8.1.2 Wellness Packages
8.2 MEDICAL SERVICES
8.3 STAYING HEALTHY

CHAPTER NINE

SUSTAINABLE TRAVEL
9.1 ECO-FRIENDLY PRACTICES
9.2 SUPPORTING LOCAL COMMUNITIES
9.3 REDUCING YOUR CARBON FOOTPRINT

CHAPTER TEN

PRACTICAL INFORMATION
10.1 LANGUAGE AND COMMUNICATION
10.2 CURRENCY AND BANKING
10.3 INTERNET AND CONNECTIVITY

10.4 SAFETY AND SECURITY
10.5 ACCESSIBILITY

CHAPTER ELEVEN

TRAVEL ITINERARIES
11.1 ONE-WEEK HIGHLIGHTS TOUR
11.2 FAMILY-FRIENDLY ADVENTURE
11.3 SOLO TRAVELER'S JOURNEY
11.4 ROMANTIC GETAWAYS
11.5 OFF-THE-BEATEN-PATH EXCURSIONS
11.6 OUTDOOR ADVENTURES

APPENDIX

USEFUL RESOURCES
A. WEBSITES AND APPS
B. CONTACT INFORMATION

DISCLAIMER

1. Prices mentioned are close approximate and may vary depending on factors such as seasonality, tour operators, and individual preferences. It's advisable to check current prices and availability before planning your visit.

2. Many travel books tend to overwhelm you with loads of pictures, right? Well, we've intentionally chosen to mix things up a bit. You might be wondering, "What's the deal?" Here's the thing: we're all about sparking your imagination, getting your curiosity going, and getting you to dive headfirst into the enchantment of Black Forest.

By leaving out the snapshots, we're nudging you to set off on an adventure powered by the thrill of the unknown. We're not just ditching visuals for the heck of it; we're aiming to give you a richer travel experience. Through our lively storytelling and in-depth insights, we'll help you visualize the breathtaking scenery, the incredible wildlife, and the rich cultural gems of Black Forest. Trust us, it's not about taking shortcuts; it's about making your journey unforgettable.

MAP BARCODE

How To Make Use Of This Barcode To Access Your Map

1. Download QR Code Scanner on your phone

2. Open the app and scan the barcode above.

3. Click on the browse options that pops up, this will take you to another page where the map of Black Forest comes up.

4. The map is ready for your use.

INTRODUCTION

A. Welcome to the Black Forest

Nestled in the heart of Europe, the Black Forest, or Schwarzwald in German, is a picturesque region famed for its dense, evergreen forests and quaint villages that evoke the timeless tales penned by the Brothers Grimm. This guide will unveil the diverse charms of the Black Forest, from the serene lakes nestled at the foothills of rolling hills to the artisanal clockmakers whose craftsmanship is revered worldwide. As you prepare to immerse yourself in the enchanting landscapes and cultural richness of this storied region, here's what to expect.

Upon your arrival, the Black Forest greets you with a landscape that stretches over 160 kilometers from north to south. Its boundaries are marked by the Rhine valley to the west and south, providing lush, fertile grounds that contrast sharply with the rugged, mountainous terrain inside the forest. Towns like Baden-Baden, Freiburg, and Triberg not only offer access to natural wonders but also embody the cultural heritage of the region with their festivals, museums, and culinary delights.

Travelers can explore a multitude of paths that weave through the forest, suitable for hiking, cycling, and in winter, cross-country skiing. The Black Forest Railway, an engineering marvel of the 19th century, offers one of the most scenic train rides in Europe, winding through tunnels and viaducts that provide spectacular views of the surrounding landscapes.

The region is also renowned for its culinary offerings, particularly the Black Forest cake, a delightful concoction of chocolate, cherries, and whipped cream, and the smoked ham that bears its name. Visitors can sample these and other local specialties at charming eateries scattered throughout the forest.

To ensure a memorable and comfortable visit, this guide will provide insights into the best times to visit, highlight top destinations, and offer tips on how to navigate local customs and travel logistics. Whether you are seeking a tranquil retreat or an adventurous exploration, the Black Black Forest welcomes you with open arms and promises an array of experiences that cater to all tastes and interests.

B. A Brief History

The Black Forest's history is as dense and fascinating as its woodlands. Initially settled in the Roman era, this region has been a pivotal crossroad in Europe, influencing and being influenced by various cultures over the centuries. It gained its name from the Roman soldiers who traversed its thick, dark woods, calling it "Silva Nigra" – the Black Forest – a name that has captivated the imagination of travelers ever since.

Throughout the Middle Ages, the Black Forest was a vital source of timber and ore, which led to the rise of vibrant market towns and the development of crafts such as glass blowing and clock making, a tradition that continues to this day with the world-famous cuckoo clocks. The forest's secluded valleys also provided refuge for monastic communities, which have left behind a legacy of historic abbeys and monasteries that dot the landscape.

The 19th century saw the Black Forest become a hotspot for the European elite who were drawn to its natural beauty and the therapeutic properties of its spa towns like Baden-Baden. This era also marked the beginning of the tourism industry in the area, with the construction of railroads and hotels catering to visitors from around the world.

The 20th century brought its challenges, particularly during the World Wars, but the post-war period saw a resurgence in the Black Forest as a tourist destination. Today, it stands as a testament to the resilience of its people and the enduring appeal of its natural beauty.

Understanding this rich tapestry of history will enhance your appreciation of the Black Forest, as every hill, valley, and village has a story to tell, contributing to the depth and allure of this unique region.

C. How to Use This Guide

This guide is structured to provide you with a comprehensive overview of the Black Forest, equipping you with all the necessary information to plan and enjoy your trip. Each chapter is devoted to different aspects of the region, from logistics like travel and accommodation to in-depth explorations of local culture and activities.

- Chapter Overview: Each chapter begins with a brief summary of its contents, allowing you to easily navigate to sections of interest.
- Detailed Descriptions: Whether you are visiting a historic site, exploring a natural wonder, or indulging in local cuisine, you will find detailed descriptions of what to expect, how to get there, and the costs involved.
- Practical Tips: From travel tips to cultural etiquette, this guide provides practical advice to help you navigate the region smoothly and respectfully.
- Local Insights: Gain insights from locals through interviews and recommendations that offer authentic

perspectives and hidden gems not commonly found in typical travel guides.
- By using this guide, you will not only be well prepared for your journey but also have the tools to explore the Black Forest with confidence and a sense of discovery. Each section is crafted to ensure you get the most value out of your visit, making your travel experience both enriching and enjoyable.

CHAPTER ONE
PLANNING YOUR TRIP

1.1 When to Visit

Seasonal Highlights

The Black Forest, known as Schwarzwald in German, is a year-round destination, each season offering its own unique charm. Here's a detailed look at what to expect during each season, along with tips on how to make the most of your visit.

1. Spring (March to May)

Spring breathes new life into the Black Forest. As the snow melts, the region transforms into a vibrant tapestry of blooming flowers and lush greenery. This season is perfect for nature lovers and outdoor enthusiasts.

Blooming Season: The Black Forest is famous for its wildflowers, particularly in April and May. Visit the smaller towns and countryside to witness fields of blooming daisies, poppies, and orchids. Triberg and its surrounding areas are particularly picturesque during this time.

Hiking: Spring is ideal for hiking. The trails are less crowded, and the weather is pleasantly cool. The Wutach Gorge, known for its stunning river views and diverse flora, offers some of the best spring hikes. The 13-kilometer (8-mile) trail through the gorge can take around 5-6 hours and is moderately challenging.

Festivals: Spring is also a time for local festivals. The Fasnacht (Carnival) in February/March is a highlight, with colorful parades and traditional costumes. Don't miss the

Freiburg Wine Festival in May, where you can sample local wines and enjoy live music.

Weather Considerations: Spring temperatures range from 10°C to 20°C (50°F to 68°F). Layers are essential as mornings and evenings can be chilly.

2. Summer (June to August)

Summer is the peak tourist season in the Black Forest. The weather is warm, making it perfect for outdoor activities and exploring the region's natural beauty.

Outdoor Activities: Summer is perfect for swimming in Lake Titisee or Schluchsee, both offering clean, refreshing water and stunning scenery. Boat rentals are available at both lakes, with prices around $15 per hour.

Cycling: The Black Forest boasts over 8,000 kilometers (5,000 miles) of cycling trails. The Southern Black Forest Cycle Route is a popular 240-kilometer (149-mile) loop that takes you through quaint villages and dense forests. Bike rentals cost about $20 per day.

Festivals: The Black Forest hosts numerous summer festivals. The Freiburg International Music Festival in July attracts classical music enthusiasts from around the world. The Black Forest Open Air Museum in Gutach also hosts traditional events showcasing local crafts, music, and cuisine.

Weather Considerations: Summer temperatures range from 20°C to 30°C (68°F to 86°F). It's advisable to book accommodations and activities in advance due to high demand.

3. Autumn (September to November)

Autumn in the Black Forest is a magical time, with the foliage transforming into vibrant shades of red, orange, and gold. This season is perfect for scenic drives and cozy experiences.

Fall Foliage: The Black Forest is renowned for its autumn colors. The Schwarzwaldhochstraße (Black Forest High Road) offers some of the best views. This scenic drive stretches for about 60 kilometers (37 miles) and takes you through dense forests and offers panoramic vistas.

Harvest Festivals: Autumn is harvest season. The region celebrates with numerous festivals such as the Apple and Pear Festival in Sasbachwalden and the Wine Harvest Festival in Oberkirch. These events feature local produce, crafts, and traditional music.

Hiking: Cooler temperatures make autumn an excellent time for hiking. The Belchen, the fourth highest mountain in the Black Forest, offers spectacular views and a variety of trails. The 4.5-kilometer (2.8-mile) summit trail is relatively easy and takes about 1.5 hours to complete.

Weather Considerations: Autumn temperatures range from 5°C to 15°C (41°F to 59°F). Pack warm clothing as temperatures can drop significantly in the evenings.

4. Winter (December to February)

Winter transforms the Black Forest into a snowy wonderland, making it a haven for winter sports enthusiasts and those seeking a cozy retreat.

Skiing and Snowboarding: The Black Forest offers numerous ski resorts. Feldberg, the highest mountain in the region, is a popular destination with over 50 kilometers (31 miles) of slopes. Ski passes cost around $35 per day for adults.

Christmas Markets: The Black Forest is famous for its traditional Christmas markets. The Freiburg Christmas Market, open from late November to December 23, features handcrafted goods, festive decorations, and local delicacies. The Baden-Baden Christmas Market is another highlight, set against the backdrop of the Kurhaus.

Spa and Wellness: Winter is perfect for indulging in the Black Forest's renowned spas. Baden-Baden is home to the luxurious Caracalla Spa and Friedrichsbad. A day pass to the Caracalla Spa costs approximately $40.

Weather Considerations: Winter temperatures range from -5°C to 5°C (23°F to 41°F). Heavy snowfall is common, so appropriate winter clothing is essential.

Weather Considerations

The Black Forest's climate can vary significantly depending on the altitude and location. Here are some key weather considerations to keep in mind when planning your trip.

Altitude: Higher altitudes, such as Feldberg and Schauinsland, experience cooler temperatures and more snowfall in winter. Lower areas, like Freiburg, have milder climates.

Rain: The Black Forest receives a fair amount of rain, especially in spring and autumn. It's wise to pack a waterproof jacket and umbrella regardless of the season.

Temperature Fluctuations: Be prepared for temperature fluctuations throughout the day. Layered clothing is recommended to adjust to varying temperatures.

1.2 Budgeting for Your Trip

Average Costs

The Black Forest offers a range of experiences to suit different budgets. Here's a breakdown of average costs to help you plan your trip.

1. Accommodation: Prices vary depending on the type of accommodation and location. On average:

- Budget: $50-$80 per night for a guesthouse or budget hotel.
- Mid-Range: $100-$150 per night for a 3-star hotel or a well-rated bed and breakfast.
- Luxury: $200-$400 per night for a 4 or 5-star hotel or a luxury resort.

2. Meals: Dining costs can vary widely. On average:

- Budget: $10-$20 for a meal at a casual restaurant or café.
- Mid-Range: $30-$50 for a meal at a mid-range restaurant.
- Luxury: $70-$120 for a meal at a high-end restaurant.

3. Transportation: Public transport is affordable and efficient. On average:

- Train Tickets: $20-$30 for a regional train ticket.
- Bus Tickets: $2-$5 per ride within towns.
- Car Rentals: $50-$70 per day for a compact car.

4. Attractions and Activities: Costs for attractions and activities can vary. On average:

- Museums and Historic Sites: $5-$15 per entry.
- Outdoor Activities (e.g., boat rentals, ski passes): $15-$40.
- Guided Tours: $50-$100 per person for a half-day tour.

Money-Saving Tips

Traveling on a budget doesn't mean missing out on the best the Black Forest has to offer. Here are some tips to help you save money while enjoying your trip.

- Travel During Shoulder Seasons: Visiting during spring (March to May) and autumn (September to November) can save you money on accommodation and activities as prices are generally lower, and there are fewer tourists.
- Use the KONUS Card: Many hotels in the Black Forest provide guests with a KONUS Card, which offers free travel on public transport throughout the region. This can save you a significant amount on transportation costs.
- Stay in Guesthouses and Bed & Breakfasts: These options often provide excellent value for money compared to hotels. They also offer a more authentic experience, often run by local families who can provide insider tips.
- Eat Like a Local: Dining at local eateries and avoiding tourist-heavy restaurants can save you money. Try the daily specials at small family-run restaurants and sample street food for affordable, delicious meals.

- Self-Cater: If you're staying in accommodation with kitchen facilities, consider buying groceries from local markets and cooking some of your meals. This can be a fun way to experience local ingredients and save money.
- Free and Low-Cost Activities: Take advantage of the numerous free outdoor activities, such as hiking, cycling, and exploring scenic towns. Many museums and attractions offer discounted or free entry on certain days.

1.3 Travel Insurance

Travel insurance is a crucial aspect of trip planning, providing peace of mind and financial protection in case of unexpected events. Here's what you need to know about purchasing travel insurance for your Black Forest adventure.

Why You Need Travel Insurance

- Medical Emergencies: Travel insurance covers medical expenses in case of illness or injury. This is especially important in a foreign country where medical costs can be high.
- Trip Cancellations: Insurance can reimburse you for non-refundable trip costs if you need to cancel due to unforeseen circumstances, such as illness, family emergencies, or natural disasters.
- Lost or Stolen Belongings: Travel insurance covers the loss or theft of your belongings, including luggage, personal items, and travel documents.
- Travel Delays: Insurance can compensate for additional expenses incurred due to travel delays or missed connections, such as accommodation and meals.

Choosing the Right Policy

When selecting a travel insurance policy, consider the following factors:

- Coverage: Ensure the policy covers medical expenses, trip cancellations, lost belongings, and travel delays. Check for any exclusions or limitations.
- Duration: Choose a policy that covers the entire duration of your trip, including any pre- or post-trip extensions.
- Activities: If you plan to engage in specific activities like skiing, hiking, or adventure sports, ensure these are covered by the policy.
- Provider Reputation: Choose a reputable insurance provider with positive customer reviews and a track record of reliable service.

How to Purchase Travel Insurance

- Online: Many insurance companies offer the convenience of purchasing policies online. Popular providers include World Nomads, Allianz, and Travel Guard.
- Travel Agents: If you're booking your trip through a travel agent, they can often arrange insurance for you.
- Credit Card Benefits: Some credit cards offer travel insurance as a benefit when you use the card to pay for your trip. Check with your credit card provider for details.

1.4 Packing Essentials

Packing appropriately for your trip to the Black Forest ensures a comfortable and enjoyable experience. Here's a detailed guide on what to pack, tailored to the region's diverse activities and changing weather conditions.

1. Clothing

- Layers: The weather in the Black Forest can be unpredictable, so layering is essential. Pack lightweight, moisture-wicking base layers, insulating mid-layers, and waterproof outer layers.
- Comfortable Footwear: Bring sturdy, comfortable shoes for hiking and walking. Waterproof hiking boots are recommended for trails, while comfortable sneakers are suitable for exploring towns.

2. Seasonal Items:

- Spring/Summer: Lightweight clothing, shorts, T-shirts, and sun protection (hat, sunglasses, sunscreen).
- Autumn/Winter: Warm clothing, including a fleece or down jacket, thermal underwear, gloves, a hat, and a scarf.
- Rain Gear: A waterproof jacket and a compact umbrella are essential, regardless of the season.

3. Accessories

- Daypack: A small backpack for day trips, hikes, and carrying essentials.
- Reusable Water Bottle: Staying hydrated is important, especially during outdoor activities. A reusable water bottle is eco-friendly and convenient.

- First Aid Kit: Include basics like band-aids, antiseptic wipes, pain relievers, and any personal medications.
- Travel Adapter: Germany uses Type C and Type F plugs. Ensure you have the appropriate travel adapter for your electronic devices.

4. Documents

- Passport: Ensure your passport is valid for at least six months beyond your planned return date.
- Travel Insurance: Carry a copy of your travel insurance policy and emergency contact numbers.
- Copies of Important Documents: Make photocopies of your passport, insurance, and any other important documents. Keep one set with you and leave another set with someone at home.
- KONUS Card: If your accommodation provides a KONUS Card for free public transport, carry it with you at all times.

5. Technology

- Smartphone and Charger: A smartphone is essential for navigation, communication, and photography. Don't forget your charger and a portable power bank.
- Camera: If you're an avid photographer, bring a camera to capture the stunning landscapes and charming towns.
- Portable Wi-Fi or SIM Card: Consider renting a portable Wi-Fi device or purchasing a local SIM card for internet access on the go.

6. Miscellaneous

- Snacks: Pack some snacks for long hikes or road trips. Energy bars, nuts, and dried fruit are great options.
- Guidebook and Maps: A good guidebook and detailed maps can be invaluable for exploring the region.
- Binoculars: For birdwatching and enjoying the panoramic views from mountain summits.
- Language Guide: A pocket-sized language guide or translation app can be helpful for communicating with locals.

By packing thoughtfully and considering the activities and weather conditions you'll encounter, you'll be well-prepared to enjoy all the Black Forest has to offer.

CHAPTER TWO
GETTING THERE AND AROUND
2.1 Arriving in the Black Forest
2.1.1 By Air

The Black Forest is accessible from several major airports, making it convenient for international travelers. The most popular entry points are Stuttgart Airport (STR) and Frankfurt Airport (FRA).

Stuttgart Airport (STR):

Located approximately 1.5 hours from the northern part of the Black Forest, Stuttgart Airport is a hub for both international and domestic flights. Major airlines like Lufthansa, British Airways, and Air France operate here, offering direct flights from numerous global destinations.

Upon arrival at Stuttgart, you can rent a car from one of the numerous rental agencies like Hertz or Sixt, conveniently located at the airport. Alternatively, take a train from Stuttgart Airport to the Black Forest. The S-Bahn (S2 and S3 lines) connects the airport to Stuttgart Central Station (Hauptbahnhof) in about 30 minutes. From there, regional trains (Deutsche Bahn) can take you to various Black Forest towns such as Freiburg, Baden-Baden, or Offenburg. A one-way train ticket from Stuttgart to Freiburg costs around $30-$40.

Frankfurt Airport (FRA):

Frankfurt Airport, one of the largest in Europe, is about 2 hours away from the Black Forest. It serves numerous airlines and offers a wide range of international flights. Upon landing, you have several options to reach the Black Forest.

The airport's long-distance train station connects directly to Deutsche Bahn's InterCity Express (ICE) services. You can take a direct train from Frankfurt Airport to cities like Karlsruhe, Baden-Baden, or Freiburg. A one-way ticket typically costs between $40-$60. Alternatively, car rentals are available at the airport, with companies like Europcar and Avis offering a range of vehicles to suit your needs.

For a more budget-friendly option, long-distance buses like FlixBus operate from both Stuttgart and Frankfurt airports, offering connections to various Black Forest towns. Bus tickets generally cost between $10-$25, depending on your destination.

2.1.2 By Train

Germany's efficient and extensive railway network makes traveling to the Black Forest by train an excellent choice. The Deutsche Bahn (DB) operates regular services connecting major German cities to the Black Forest region.

From Stuttgart

Stuttgart Hauptbahnhof (Main Station) is a major railway hub, offering frequent connections to the Black Forest. Deutsche Bahn (DB) operates these services, ensuring comfort and efficiency.

Destinations and Routes

1. Offenburg:

- Journey Duration: Approximately 1 hour
- Ticket Price: $30-$40
- Route: Direct Regional-Express (RE) or InterCity (IC) trains

Offenburg serves as the gateway to the central Black Forest. From here, you can explore charming towns and picturesque landscapes. The town itself boasts beautiful baroque architecture and vibrant local markets.

2. Triberg:

- Journey Duration: Approximately 2 hours
- Ticket Price: $30-$40
- Route: Take a train from Stuttgart to Offenburg, then transfer to a regional train to Triberg.

Triberg is famous for its stunning waterfalls, the highest in Germany. The town also offers a fascinating look at the traditional craft of cuckoo clock making. The Black Forest Museum provides insights into local history and culture.

3. Freiburg im Breisgau:

- Journey Duration: Approximately 2 hours
- Ticket Price: $30-$40
- Route: Direct InterCity Express (ICE) or InterCity (IC) trains

Freiburg, known for its medieval architecture and sunny climate, is a must-visit. The Freiburg Minster, a magnificent Gothic cathedral, dominates the cityscape. The vibrant Old Town, with its cobbled streets and colorful market squares, is perfect for leisurely strolls.

Booking Tips

Tickets can be purchased online via the Deutsche Bahn website, at station ticket counters, or using DB's mobile app. Booking in advance often yields discounts. Consider purchasing a regional pass like the Baden-Württemberg-

Ticket, which offers unlimited travel for a day within the state for about $25-$30.

Amenities

Stuttgart Hauptbahnhof offers various amenities including shops, restaurants, and lounges. The DB Lounge, available to first-class passengers and BahnCard holders, provides a comfortable space to relax before your journey. Onboard amenities include free Wi-Fi, power outlets, and a bistro car for refreshments.

From Frankfurt

Frankfurt Hauptbahnhof (Main Station) is one of the busiest in Europe, offering excellent connectivity to the Black Forest.

Destinations and Routes

1. Karlsruhe:

- Journey Duration: Approximately 1.5 hours
- Ticket Price: $40-$50
- Route: Direct InterCity Express (ICE) or InterCity (IC) trains

Karlsruhe is a vibrant city known for its fan-shaped layout and grand palace. The Karlsruhe Palace, with its extensive gardens and museum, is a highlight. The city also serves as a gateway to the northern Black Forest.

2. Baden-Baden:

- Journey Duration: Approximately 1.5 hours
- Ticket Price: $40-$50
- Route: Direct InterCity Express (ICE) or InterCity (IC) trains

Baden-Baden is renowned for its luxurious thermal spas and elegant casino. The Friedrichsbad and Caracalla Spa offer rejuvenating thermal baths, while the Kurhaus hosts concerts and cultural events.

3. Freiburg im Breisgau:

- Journey Duration: Approximately 2.5 hours
- Ticket Price: $40-$60
- Route: Direct InterCity Express (ICE) trains

As mentioned earlier, Freiburg is a charming city with a rich cultural heritage. Don't miss the chance to explore its vibrant markets and picturesque neighborhoods.

Booking Tips

Like Stuttgart, tickets can be booked via the Deutsche Bahn website, mobile app, or at station counters. Advance bookings often come with significant discounts. The Baden-Württemberg-Ticket is also valid for travel from Frankfurt, offering great value for money.

Amenities

Frankfurt Hauptbahnhof is well-equipped with shops, restaurants, and lounges. The DB Lounge provides a comfortable waiting area for first-class passengers. Onboard amenities on ICE trains include free Wi-Fi, power outlets, and a restaurant car.

2.1.3 By Car

Driving to the Black Forest offers flexibility and the opportunity to explore the region at your own pace. Germany's well-maintained Autobahns and scenic byways provide a pleasurable driving experience.

From Stuttgart:

The journey from Stuttgart to the northern Black Forest towns like Baden-Baden or Freudenstadt takes about 1-1.5 hours via the A81 Autobahn. For Freiburg, located further south, the drive takes approximately 2 hours via the A8 and A5 Autobahns.

From Frankfurt:

The drive from Frankfurt to the Black Forest can take 2-3 hours, depending on your destination. For instance, Baden-Baden is about a 2-hour drive via the A5, while Freiburg is closer to 3 hours along the same route.

Car Rentals:

Major rental companies like Hertz, Avis, and Sixt have branches at both Stuttgart and Frankfurt airports, as well as in city centers. Prices for a compact car start at around $40-$60 per day, with larger vehicles and premium options available at higher rates.

Driving Tips:

Ensure you have a valid driver's license and consider an international driving permit if necessary. Familiarize yourself with German traffic rules and signage, and always keep some cash on hand for parking fees and tolls. Many hotels and accommodations offer parking facilities, either free or for a nominal fee.

2.2 Navigating the Region

2.2.1 Public Transportation

The Black Forest region boasts an efficient and well-connected public transportation network, making it easy to explore without a car.

Trains

Deutsche Bahn:

Germany's national railway company, Deutsche Bahn (DB), operates a comprehensive network of regional trains throughout the Black Forest. The trains are known for their punctuality, cleanliness, and comfort, offering a reliable way to travel between major towns and smaller villages.

Schwarzwaldbahn:

One of the most scenic railway lines in Germany, the Schwarzwaldbahn (Black Forest Railway) runs from Offenburg to Singen, passing through picturesque towns like Hausach, Triberg, and St. Georgen. This route offers stunning views of the dense forest, rolling hills, and charming villages that define the region.

- Offenburg to Triberg: The journey from Offenburg to Triberg takes about 1 hour and 15 minutes. The Triberg station is conveniently located near the famous Triberg Waterfalls, one of Germany's highest waterfalls. A one-way ticket costs approximately $15.
- Triberg to Villingen: Continuing from Triberg to Villingen takes around 40 minutes. Villingen's old town, with its medieval gates and historic buildings, is a must-visit. A one-way ticket costs about $10.
- Villingen to Singen: The final stretch from Villingen to Singen takes about 1 hour and offers breathtaking views of the Wutach Valley. A one-way ticket costs roughly $20.

Booking Tickets:

Tickets can be purchased at train stations from ticket machines or counters, or online via the Deutsche Bahn website and mobile app. For those planning extensive travel within the region, the Baden-Württemberg-Ticket offers unlimited travel for a day within the state for about $25-$30. This ticket is valid on all regional trains, buses, and trams, making it an excellent value for money.

KONUS Card:

Many hotels and guesthouses in the Black Forest provide the KONUS Card to their guests. This card allows free travel on regional trains and buses throughout the Black Forest. It's a fantastic perk that can save you a significant amount of money on transportation. Simply show your KONUS Card to the conductor or bus driver to enjoy free rides.

Buses

Local Bus Services:

Local bus services complement the train network, providing access to smaller villages and attractions not served by trains. The buses are well-maintained, punctual, and cover a vast area, making it easy to explore the entire region.

- Südbadenbus Network: This network covers the southern Black Forest, including towns like Freiburg, Titisee, and Hinterzarten. The buses are frequent, with schedules designed to connect seamlessly with train services. For example, from Freiburg, you can take a bus to Titisee in about 40 minutes for around $5.
- Ortenau-S-Bahn: This bus service covers the northern Black Forest, including towns like Offenburg, Baden-Baden, and Freudenstadt. It's an excellent option for reaching destinations like the Mummelsee Lake and the All Saints Waterfalls.

Timetables and Routes:

Bus timetables are available at bus stops, tourist information centers, and online. The DB Navigator app also includes bus schedules, making it a convenient tool for planning your journeys. Routes are well-marked, and most bus stops have clear signage indicating the destination and departure times.

Fares:

Bus fares are affordable, typically costing $2-$5 per journey. Day passes and multi-ride tickets are available, offering further savings for frequent travelers. The KONUS Card, mentioned earlier, is also valid on most regional buses, providing free travel for cardholders.

Tram Services

Freiburg:

Freiburg boasts an extensive and efficient tram network, making it easy to get around the city and its immediate surroundings. The trams are modern, frequent, and an integral part of the city's public transportation system.

- Tram Lines: Freiburg's tram network consists of several lines (1, 2, 3, 4, 5), each serving different parts of the city. For example, Line 1 connects the central train station (Hauptbahnhof) to the western district of Landwasser, passing through the historic Old Town and the university area.
- Fares: A single tram ticket in Freiburg costs around $3, and can be purchased at tram stops or via the VAG Freiburg app. Day passes are available for about $6-$8, offering unlimited travel within the city for a day.

Regional Trams:

In addition to Freiburg, other towns in the Black Forest, such as Karlsruhe, also have tram services that connect the city center with suburban areas and neighboring towns. These regional trams are a convenient way to explore the area.

Timetables and Apps:

Timetables for trams are available at stops, tourist information centers, and online. The VAG Freiburg app is particularly useful for real-time information on tram schedules, routes, and ticket purchases.

Useful Tips for Public Transportation

1. Planning Your Routes:

Using public transportation in the Black Forest is straightforward with a bit of planning. Tourist information centers, hotel reception desks, and local websites provide valuable resources for planning your journeys. The DB Navigator app and local transportation apps like VAG Freiburg are indispensable tools, offering real-time schedules, route maps, and ticket purchasing options.

2. Language:

While German is the primary language, many signs, and announcements are also in English, especially in tourist areas. Most train and bus station staff speak basic English and are usually very helpful.

3. Punctuality:

German public transportation is known for its punctuality. Trains and buses generally run on time, so be sure to arrive at the station or stop a few minutes early. If you miss a connection, there's usually another service shortly after.

4. Accessibility:

Public transportation in the Black Forest is generally accessible for travelers with disabilities. Many trains and buses are equipped with ramps and designated spaces for wheelchairs. Stations and stops often have elevators and other facilities to assist passengers with mobility issues.

5. Comfort:

Trains, buses, and trams in the Black Forest are well-maintained and offer a comfortable ride. Most services have ample seating, and many trains offer first-class options for an even more comfortable journey. Public transportation is also equipped with free Wi-Fi on some routes, making it easy to stay connected during your travels.

6. Cost-Effective Travel:

Using public transportation is a cost-effective way to explore the Black Forest. The KONUS Card, regional passes like the Baden-Württemberg-Ticket, and day passes for buses and trams provide excellent value for money, allowing you to travel extensively without breaking the bank.

Key Destinations Accessible by Public Transportation

1. Freiburg im Breisgau:

- Train: Freiburg is a major hub with frequent train connections to other Black Forest towns and cities across Germany. The main train station is centrally located, providing easy access to the Old Town and other attractions.

- Tram: The city's tram network is excellent for getting around Freiburg. Key stops include the central train station, Bertoldsbrunnen in the heart of the Old Town, and the university area.
- Bus: Regional buses connect Freiburg with nearby towns like Titisee, Hinterzarten, and Staufen, offering an easy way to explore the surrounding areas.

2. Baden-Baden:

- Train: Direct trains from Karlsruhe and Stuttgart make Baden-Baden easily accessible. The main train station is a short bus ride from the city center and the famous thermal spas.
- Bus: Local buses connect the train station with the city center, thermal spas, and other attractions. Bus route 201 is particularly useful for reaching the spa district.

3. Triberg:

- Train: Triberg is served by the Schwarzwaldbahn, with direct connections to Offenburg and Singen. The train station is a short walk from the Triberg Waterfalls and the town center.
- Bus: Local buses connect Triberg with surrounding villages and attractions. The bus to Schonach, home of the world's largest cuckoo clock, is a popular route.

4. Titisee-Neustadt:

- Train: Regional trains connect Titisee-Neustadt with Freiburg and Donaueschingen. The station in Titisee is close to the lake, making it convenient for visitors.
- Bus: Local buses provide access to nearby attractions like the Feldberg Mountain and the Badeparadies

Schwarzwald water park. The bus from Titisee to the Feldberg summit is a favorite for hikers and winter sports enthusiasts.

5. Offenburg:

- Train: Offenburg is a major railway hub with connections to Freiburg, Karlsruhe, and Strasbourg. It's an ideal starting point for exploring the northern Black Forest.
- Bus: The Ortenau-S-Bahn bus network connects Offenburg with nearby towns and attractions. Buses to Gengenbach, known for its charming old town and festive Christmas market, are particularly popular.

By leveraging the well-connected and efficient public transportation network, travelers can easily explore the Black Forest's stunning landscapes, historic towns, and hidden gems.

2.2.2 Car Rentals

Renting a car provides unparalleled flexibility and the chance to explore the Black Forest's hidden gems.

Rental Locations

Car rental services are widely available throughout the Black Forest, with major rental agencies operating at airports, train stations, and city centers.

1. Airport Rentals:

The most convenient places to rent a car are at Stuttgart Airport (STR) and Frankfurt Airport (FRA). Both airports host several car rental companies, including Europcar, Avis, Hertz, Sixt, and Enterprise. Rental desks are located in the arrivals hall, making it easy to pick up your car as soon as you land.

2. Train Station Rentals:

For those arriving by train, car rentals are available at major train stations in cities such as Freiburg, Baden-Baden, and Offenburg. Renting from a train station is a good option if you prefer to take public transport to a central location before picking up a car.

3. City Center Rentals:

Many towns and cities within the Black Forest, including Triberg, Titisee-Neustadt, and Freudenstadt, have local car rental offices. These can be a convenient option if you're already in the region and decide you want a car for a few days to explore further.

Costs and Requirements

1. Rental Costs:

The cost of renting a car in the Black Forest varies depending on the type of vehicle, rental duration, and time of year. On average, expect to pay around $40-$60 per day for a compact car, $60-$80 for a mid-sized vehicle, and $100 or more for luxury or larger vehicles. Weekly rental rates are often more economical, with prices starting at around $250 for a compact car.

2. Insurance:

Basic insurance is typically included in the rental price, covering liability and theft. However, it's advisable to consider additional coverage options, such as Collision Damage Waiver (CDW) and Super CDW, to reduce your financial liability in case of an accident. Full insurance coverage can add $10-$20 per day to your rental cost.

3. Requirements:

To rent a car in the Black Forest, you'll need a valid driver's license. If your license is not in English or German, an International Driving Permit (IDP) is recommended. Most rental companies require drivers to be at least 21 years old, with a minimum of one year of driving experience. Drivers under 25 may be subject to a young driver surcharge, typically around $15-$25 per day.

4. Payment:

A major credit card is usually required to secure a rental. Debit cards are accepted by some companies but often come with additional restrictions. Be sure to check the payment policies of your chosen rental agency in advance.

Driving Routes and Scenic Drives

The Black Forest is renowned for its picturesque landscapes, charming villages, and winding roads. Here are some of the most scenic drives you can enjoy with your rental car:

1. Schwarzwaldhochstraße (Black Forest High Road):

One of the most famous driving routes in the Black Forest, the Schwarzwaldhochstraße stretches from Baden-Baden to Freudenstadt. This 60-kilometer route offers stunning views of the Rhine Valley, dense forests, and the highest peaks of the northern Black Forest. Highlights along the way include the picturesque Mummelsee Lake, the All Saints Waterfalls, and the historic Black Forest Open Air Museum in Gutach.

Plan for at least half a day to explore this route, with plenty of stops for photos and short hikes.

2. Badische Weinstraße (Baden Wine Road):

For wine enthusiasts, the Badische Weinstraße offers a delightful journey through the region's vineyards and wine villages. This route runs from Baden-Baden to Weil am Rhein, passing through Ortenau, Kaiserstuhl, and Markgräflerland wine regions. Visit charming towns like Sasbachwalden, known for its half-timbered houses and local wineries, or stop by the historic town of Gengenbach, famous for its annual Christmas market. Many wineries offer tours and tastings, so take your time to savor the local flavors.

3. Scenic Route Through the Southern Black Forest:

Begin your journey in Freiburg, a vibrant university town with a stunning Gothic cathedral and a bustling market square. From Freiburg, drive south to the picturesque town of Staufen, known for its ruined castle and historical significance as the final residence of alchemist Johann Georg Faust. Continue to Bad Krozingen, a spa town with thermal baths perfect for relaxation. Your final stop could be the charming town of Titisee-Neustadt, home to the beautiful Lake Titisee, where you can enjoy boat rides, lakeside cafes, and hiking trails.

Other Notable Drives:

- Kinzigtal Valley: Explore the heart of the Black Forest along the Kinzigtal Valley, visiting towns like Haslach

and Wolfach, known for their traditional Black Forest architecture and heritage.
- Feldberg Drive: Head towards the Feldberg, the highest mountain in the Black Forest, offering panoramic views, ski resorts, and hiking trails.

Parking

Parking in the Black Forest is generally straightforward, with various options available in towns, cities, and near major attractions.

1. Town and City Parking:

Most towns have public parking lots and garages, with rates ranging from $1-$2 per hour. Freiburg, for example, offers several centrally located parking garages such as the Schlossberg Garage (Schlossbergstraße, 79098 Freiburg), which charges around $2 per hour or $15 per day.

2. Hotel Parking:

Many hotels offer guest parking, either for free or a small fee. It's advisable to confirm parking availability when booking your accommodation. Hotels in smaller towns often provide complimentary parking, while those in busier areas might charge $5-$10 per day.

3. Attraction Parking:

Major tourist attractions like the Triberg Waterfalls and the Black Forest Open Air Museum have designated parking areas. Parking fees vary, typically costing $2-$5 for a few hours. Always check the signage for payment instructions, as some locations may require coins or a parking app.

4. Driving Tips

Driving in the Black Forest can be a delightful experience, but it's essential to be aware of local driving regulations and practices.

Speed Limits:

- Urban areas: 50 km/h (31 mph)
- Rural roads: 100 km/h (62 mph)
- Autobahns: No general speed limit, but 130 km/h (81 mph) is recommended

5. Road Conditions:

The Black Forest's roads are well-maintained, but some rural areas can be narrow and winding. Always drive cautiously, especially in winter when snow and ice are common. Winter tires are mandatory from October to April.

6. Navigation:

While GPS is invaluable for navigation, consider bringing a paper map as a backup. Mobile reception can be spotty in remote areas. Many car rental companies offer GPS units for an additional fee, typically around $10 per day.

7. Fuel:

Fuel prices in Germany are higher than in some other countries, averaging around $6-$7 per gallon. Most gas stations accept credit cards, but it's wise to have some cash on hand. Diesel vehicles are popular and often more fuel-efficient for long drives.

8. Etiquette:

- Use turn signals when changing lanes or turning.

- Yield to pedestrians at crosswalks.
- Be aware of cyclists, especially in towns and villages.
- Parking on sidewalks is prohibited unless specifically marked.

2.2.3 Cycling and Hiking

The Black Forest is a paradise for outdoor enthusiasts, with an extensive network of cycling and hiking trails.

Cycling in the Black Forest

Overview of Cycling Routes

The Black Forest boasts an extensive network of cycling routes that cover diverse terrains, from gentle paths suitable for families to demanding trails for experienced cyclists. Here are some of the top cycling routes to explore:

1. Südschwarzwald-Radweg (Southern Black Forest Cycle Path)

- Route Description: This 240-kilometer circular route starts and ends in Freiburg, taking you through scenic valleys, dense forests, and idyllic villages. The route is well-marked and suitable for all levels.
- Highlights: Pass through the Wutach Gorge, Lake Titisee, and the vineyards of the Markgräflerland region. Enjoy panoramic views from the Höchenschwand plateau and explore charming towns like St. Blasien and Bonndorf.
- Practical Information: Bike rentals are available in Freiburg, with daily rates around $15-$25. Accommodation options range from guesthouses to luxury hotels, with prices varying accordingly.

2. Badische Weinstraße (Baden Wine Road)

- Route Description: This route winds through the vineyards of the Baden wine region, offering a blend of natural beauty and cultural experiences. Starting in Baden-Baden, it stretches south to Weil am Rhein near the Swiss border.
- Highlights: Visit renowned wineries, sample local wines, and enjoy the picturesque landscapes. Key stops include the towns of Offenburg, Oberkirch, and Freiburg.
- Practical Information: Many towns along the route offer bike rentals and wine tasting tours. Accommodation ranges from quaint inns to luxurious resorts, with prices from $50 to $200 per night.

3. Kinzig Valley Cycle Path

- Route Description: Following the course of the Kinzig River, this 95-kilometer route takes you from the town of Lossburg to Offenburg. The path is mostly flat and suitable for families and leisurely cyclists.
- Highlights: Explore historic towns like Schiltach, known for its half-timbered houses, and Gengenbach, with its beautiful town square. The route offers numerous picnic spots and scenic viewpoints.
- Practical Information: Bike rentals are available in Lossburg and Offenburg. Along the route, you'll find a variety of accommodation options, including family-friendly guesthouses and mid-range hotels.

Tips for Cycling in the Black Forest

- Planning Your Route: Before setting out, plan your route based on your fitness level and interests. Maps and guides are available at local tourist offices and online.

- Bike Rentals: Rental services are widely available in major towns and tourist centers. Prices typically range from $15 to $25 per day, with discounts for longer rentals.
- Safety Gear: Always wear a helmet and carry essential safety gear, including a repair kit, first aid supplies, and a map. Reflective clothing and lights are recommended for low-light conditions.
- Weather Considerations: The weather can change rapidly in the Black Forest. Check the forecast before your ride and be prepared for rain or cooler temperatures, especially at higher elevations.
- Local Etiquette: Respect local customs and the natural environment. Stick to designated trails, avoid littering, and be considerate of other cyclists and pedestrians.

Hiking in the Black Forest

Overview of Hiking Trails

The Black Forest is a hiker's paradise, offering trails that range from easy walks to challenging multi-day treks. Here are some of the most popular hiking routes:

1. Westweg Trail

Route Description: The Westweg is a famous long-distance trail that stretches 285 kilometers from Pforzheim in the north to Basel in the south. It is divided into 12 stages, each offering unique landscapes and experiences.

- Highlights: Hike through dense forests, over rolling hills, and along scenic ridges. Key sights include the Feldberg, the highest peak in the Black Forest, the

stunning Titisee lake, and the picturesque town of St. Blasien.
- Practical Information: The trail is well-marked with red diamonds. Accommodation options range from rustic huts to comfortable guesthouses. Budget around $30-$50 per night for lodging. Many hikers complete the trail in 12-14 days, but shorter sections can be enjoyed as well.

2. Triberg Waterfalls and Nature Trail

- Route Description: This short, family-friendly trail leads to Germany's highest waterfalls in Triberg. The trail is easy to navigate and suitable for all ages.
- Highlights: Experience the impressive 163-meter high Triberg Waterfalls and explore the surrounding nature park. The area is rich in flora and fauna, with several scenic viewpoints and picnic areas.
- Practical Information: The entrance fee to the waterfalls is around $5 for adults and $3 for children. The trail is open year-round, with well-maintained paths and informative signs along the way. Nearby parking is available for a small fee.

3. Feldberg Summit Trail

- Route Description: This moderate to challenging hike takes you to the summit of Feldberg, the highest mountain in the Black Forest at 1,493 meters. The trail starts at the Feldberg Pass and loops around the summit.
- Highlights: Enjoy panoramic views of the Black Forest, the Swiss Alps, and the Vosges Mountains. The trail passes through diverse landscapes, including alpine meadows, forests, and rocky outcrops.

- Practical Information: The trail is well-marked, and the hike to the summit and back takes about 4-5 hours. Wear sturdy hiking boots and bring plenty of water and snacks. In winter, the area is popular for skiing and snowshoeing.

Tips for Hiking in the Black Forest

- Choosing the Right Trail: Select a trail that matches your fitness level and interests. Local tourist offices provide detailed maps and guides, and many trails are well-signposted.
- Essential Gear: Carry essential hiking gear, including a map, compass, first aid kit, and sufficient water and snacks. Wear appropriate clothing and sturdy hiking boots.
- Weather Preparedness: The weather can be unpredictable, especially at higher elevations. Check the forecast before heading out and be prepared for rain, wind, or sudden temperature drops.

Trail Etiquette: Respect the natural environment and local customs. Stay on marked trails, take your litter with you, and be considerate of wildlife and other hikers.

Safety Considerations: Inform someone of your hiking plans and expected return time. Mobile reception can be spotty in remote areas, so consider carrying a whistle or other signaling device in case of emergencies.

CHAPTER THREE
TOP DESTINATIONS
3.1 Freiburg im Breisgau
3.1.1 City Overview

Freiburg im Breisgau, often simply referred to as Freiburg, is a gem in the heart of the Black Forest. This vibrant city is known for its medieval architecture, sun-drenched climate, and an unmistakable charm that attracts visitors year-round. With a population of around 230,000, Freiburg seamlessly blends historic charm with a lively, youthful atmosphere, thanks in part to its large student population from the University of Freiburg.

The city is noted for its commitment to sustainability and green living. It boasts an impressive network of cycling paths and is considered one of Germany's most bike-friendly cities. Freiburg's old town, with its cobblestone streets, is best explored on foot or by bicycle. The city is surrounded by lush forests and vineyards, offering countless opportunities for outdoor activities and excursions.

Freiburg's climate is one of the warmest in Germany, often earning it the title of the country's "sunniest city." This favorable weather makes it an ideal destination for outdoor dining, leisurely strolls, and enjoying its many parks and gardens. The Münsterplatz, the city's main square, is a bustling hub where locals and tourists gather to shop at the farmers' market or enjoy a meal at one of the many cafés.

Freiburg is a gateway to the Black Forest, making it an excellent base for exploring the region. Its well-preserved medieval architecture, vibrant cultural scene, and friendly locals make it a must-visit destination for any traveler to the Black Forest.

3.1.2 Must-See Attractions

1. Freiburg Minster (Münsterplatz 1, 79098 Freiburg im Breisgau, Germany)

The Freiburg Minster, a magnificent Gothic cathedral, stands as the crown jewel of Freiburg's skyline. Its construction began in 1200 and took nearly three centuries to complete, resulting in a stunning blend of architectural styles. The Minster's 116-meter-high tower, often hailed as one of the most beautiful spires in Christendom, dominates the cityscape and offers breathtaking views over Freiburg and the surrounding Black Forest.

Visiting Details: The cathedral is open daily from 10 AM to 5 PM, and entry is free, although donations are welcome. Guided tours are available for about $12 per person and offer deeper insights into the history, architecture, and art of the Minster.

Tips: Climbing the tower is a must-do activity for those who can manage the steep and narrow steps. The climb is strenuous, but the panoramic views from the top are worth every step. On a clear day, you can see as far as the Vosges Mountains in France. If you're visiting in the morning, plan your climb early to avoid the midday heat and the crowds. Don't miss the daily market in the Münsterplatz, where you can buy fresh produce, local crafts, and enjoy a quick snack from one of the many food stalls.

2. Schlossberg (Schloßbergring, 79098 Freiburg im Breisgau, Germany)

Schlossberg, or "Castle Hill," is a lush green hill that rises to the east of Freiburg's old town, offering a perfect blend of nature and history. Historically, it was the site of a medieval castle, and today it serves as a popular recreational area with walking trails, panoramic viewpoints, and historical ruins.

Visiting Details: Schlossberg is accessible year-round and free to visit. The Schlossbergbahn funicular railway, which operates from 9 AM to 9 PM, offers a quick and scenic ride to the top for about $5 for a round trip.

Tips: Start your visit at the Kanonenplatz, a popular viewpoint halfway up the hill. From there, continue to the top of the Schlossberg, where you'll find the ruins of old fortifications and the Aussichtsturm, a modern observation tower that offers even more spectacular views. The beer garden at the top is a great spot to relax with a cold drink and a traditional German snack. If you're up for more exploration, several trails lead from the Schlossberg into the surrounding Black Forest, providing opportunities for longer hikes.

3. Münsterplatz (Münsterplatz, 79098 Freiburg im Breisgau, Germany)

Münsterplatz is the beating heart of Freiburg, a bustling square surrounded by historic buildings and dominated by the imposing Freiburg Minster. It's a lively gathering place where locals and tourists mingle, especially during the daily farmers' market.

Visiting Details: The market operates every morning except Sundays, from 7 AM to 1 PM. It's an excellent opportunity to sample local produce, meats, cheeses, and handcrafted goods.

Tips: The "Lange Rote," a long, spicy sausage, is a must-try. You can find it at various market stalls for around $4. The Münsterplatz is also a great place to people-watch while enjoying a coffee or a pastry from one of the nearby cafés. During the Advent season, the square transforms into a magical Christmas market, with festive stalls selling holiday treats, decorations, and crafts.

4. Freiburg's Bächle (Throughout the Old Town)

The Bächle are a unique and charming feature of Freiburg's old town. These small water-filled runnels date back to the Middle Ages and originally served as a water supply and fire prevention system. Today, they add a distinctive character to the city's streets.

Tips: The Bächle are shallow enough for children to splash around in during the summer, and you'll often see locals and their dogs cooling off in them. Be careful not to step into one accidentally, as it's a local legend that if you do, you'll marry a Freiburger! On hot days, the cool water provides a refreshing contrast to the warm stone streets, making a stroll through the old town even more enjoyable.

5. Augustiner Museum (Gerberau 15, 79098 Freiburg im Breisgau, Germany)

Housed in a former monastery, the Augustiner Museum is a treasure trove of art and history. Its collections include medieval sculpture, Baroque paintings, and a stunning array of stained glass windows from the Freiburg Minster.

Visiting Details: Open Tuesday to Sunday from 10 AM to 5 PM. Admission is approximately $10 for adults, with discounts available for students and seniors.

Tips: The museum's layout allows for a leisurely and immersive experience. Start with the impressive medieval art collection on the ground floor, then move up to the Baroque paintings and modern art exhibits. The top floor offers an excellent view of the surrounding rooftops and the Black Forest beyond. Plan to spend at least two hours exploring the museum's varied collections.

6. Schwabentor (Schwabentor, 79098 Freiburg im Breisgau, Germany)

The Schwabentor, or Swabian Gate, is one of two remaining medieval gates in Freiburg. Built in the 13th century, it features a colorful mural depicting a Swabian merchant. The gate once marked the city's southern boundary and is now a picturesque landmark at the entrance to the old town.

Visiting Details: Open daily and free to visit. The area around the Schwabentor is perfect for a leisurely stroll, with charming shops, cafés, and historic buildings.

Tips: The gate is beautifully illuminated at night, making it a great spot for evening photography. Nearby, you'll find the Schwabentorbrücke, a small bridge with lovely views of the surrounding area. This part of town is also home to some of Freiburg's best-preserved medieval architecture, so take your time to explore the narrow streets and hidden courtyards.

7. Martinstor (Martinstor, 79098 Freiburg im Breisgau, Germany)

The Martinstor, or Martin's Gate, is the oldest of Freiburg's two remaining city gates. It was built in the early 13th century and later modified with a Baroque-style tower in the 17th century. The gate is a prominent landmark and a gateway to the bustling shopping street, Kaiser-Joseph-Straße.

Visiting Details: Open daily and free to visit. The surrounding area is vibrant with shops, restaurants, and street performers.

Tips: Climb the steps to the top of the gate for a unique perspective of the old town and the bustling streets below. The nearby Bertoldsbrunnen tram stop is a major hub for public transport, making the Martinstor an easy meeting point for exploring the city. After visiting the gate, take a stroll along Kaiser-Joseph-Straße, Freiburg's main shopping street, lined with a mix of high-end boutiques, department stores, and local shops.

8. Seepark Betzenhausen (Falkenbergerstraße, 79110 Freiburg im Breisgau, Germany)

Seepark Betzenhausen is a sprawling urban park located west of Freiburg's city center. It features a large lake, beautiful gardens, and extensive recreational facilities, making it a perfect spot for relaxation and outdoor activities.

Visiting Details: Open daily from dawn to dusk and free to visit. The park is easily accessible by tram and offers ample parking for those arriving by car.

Tips: Rent a paddleboat to explore the lake, which costs around $10 per hour. The park's Japanese Garden is a serene spot for a quiet walk or meditation. During the summer months, the park hosts various festivals and events, including outdoor concerts and food markets. Bring a picnic and enjoy a leisurely afternoon by the lake, or visit one of the park's cafés for a light meal.

9. Mundenhof (Mundenhofer Str. 37, 79111 Freiburg im Breisgau, Germany)

Mundenhof is Freiburg's largest animal park and a popular family destination. It offers a mix of domestic and exotic animals in spacious enclosures, providing an educational and enjoyable experience for visitors of all ages.

Visiting Details: Open daily from 9 AM to 6 PM. Admission is free, but donations are encouraged to support the park's upkeep and animal care.

Tips: The park's layout is easy to navigate, with well-marked trails and plenty of shaded areas for hot days. Don't miss the opportunity to feed some of the animals; feed bags are available for a small fee. The park also features a playground and picnic areas, making it an ideal spot for a family outing. Plan to spend at least half a day exploring the various exhibits and enjoying the park's amenities.

10. Vauban District (Vauban, 79100 Freiburg im Breisgau, Germany)

Vauban is a unique and innovative neighborhood known for its commitment to sustainability and eco-friendly living. Built on the site of a former French military base, Vauban has become a model for sustainable urban development.

Visiting Details: The district is open to the public, and guided tours are available for around $15 per person. Tours typically last about two hours and provide insights into the district's design and sustainable practices.

Tips: Explore the area on foot or by bike to fully appreciate its innovative design. Highlights include the solar village, where houses generate more energy than they consume, and the car-free zones that promote walking and cycling. Visit one of the district's cafés or organic food stores to experience the local lifestyle. If you're interested in sustainable living and urban planning, Vauban is a must-see.

3.1.3 Dining and Accommodation
Dining in Freiburg

Freiburg is a haven for food enthusiasts, offering a variety of dining experiences from traditional German fare to international cuisine. The city's culinary scene is a reflection of its rich cultural heritage and modern vibrancy. Here are some must-visit dining spots in Freiburg:

1. Hausbrauerei Feierling (Gerberau 46, 79098 Freiburg im Breisgau, Germany)

- Overview: A beloved local brewery, Hausbrauerei Feierling offers a fantastic selection of beers brewed on-site, accompanied by hearty German dishes. The atmosphere is relaxed and welcoming, making it a favorite among both locals and tourists.
- Menu Highlights: Be sure to try the "Schwarzwald Flammkuchen," a local flatbread topped with cheese, onions, and Black Forest ham. Pair it with one of their house-brewed beers, like the Feierling Inselhopf. The average cost for a meal with a beer is around $20-$30 per person.
- Opening Hours: Daily from 11 AM to midnight. Given its popularity, it's wise to make a reservation, especially on weekends.
- Tips: Enjoy your meal in the beer garden if the weather is nice. The lively outdoor space adds to the overall experience, offering a great view of the Gerberau canal.

2. Gasthaus zum Kranz (Gerberau 26, 79098 Freiburg im Breisgau, Germany)

- Overview: This traditional German restaurant is known for its cozy atmosphere and delicious regional cuisine. It's a great place to experience authentic Black Forest dishes.
- Menu Highlights: The "Schweinshaxe" (pork knuckle) is a must-try, as well as the "Käsespätzle" (cheese noodles). The restaurant also offers seasonal specialties and a variety of regional wines. Expect to spend around $15-$25 per person.
- Opening Hours: Open Tuesday to Sunday from 11:30 AM to 2:30 PM and 5:30 PM to 10 PM. Closed on Mondays.
- Tips: The portions are generous, so consider sharing dishes if you're not too hungry. The restaurant's location in the historic old town adds to its charm.

3. Wolfshöhle (Konviktstraße 8, 79098 Freiburg im Breisgau, Germany)

- Overview: For a fine dining experience, Wolfshöhle offers gourmet cuisine in an elegant setting. The restaurant has received accolades for its innovative dishes and excellent service.
- Menu Highlights: Opt for the tasting menu to enjoy a variety of seasonal dishes crafted with fresh, local ingredients. The average cost for a three-course meal is around $60-$80 per person.
- Opening Hours: Open Tuesday to Saturday from 6 PM to midnight. Reservations are recommended.
- Tips: Dress smartly to match the upscale ambiance. The restaurant's wine list is extensive, so ask for

pairing recommendations to enhance your dining experience.

4. Kaiser's Gute Backstube (Schwarzwaldstraße 78, 79117 Freiburg im Breisgau, Germany)

- Overview: A popular bakery chain in the region, Kaiser's Gute Backstube is perfect for a quick bite or a relaxed breakfast. Their freshly baked goods and pastries are a treat.
- Menu Highlights: Try their pretzels, Black Forest cake, and a variety of breads. A typical breakfast or snack costs around $5-$10.
- Opening Hours: Daily from 6 AM to 6 PM.
- Tips: Ideal for a quick breakfast before heading out to explore the city. Their coffee is excellent and pairs perfectly with any of their pastries.

5. Dattler Schlossbergrestaurant (Am Schlossberg 1, 79104 Freiburg im Breisgau, Germany)

- Overview: Located on Schlossberg hill, this restaurant offers stunning views of Freiburg along with its fine dining options. It's a great spot for a special occasion or a romantic dinner.
- Menu Highlights: The menu features a mix of local and international dishes. Their seasonal specialties and extensive wine list are highlights. Expect to spend around $40-$60 per person.
- Opening Hours: Open daily from 11:30 AM to 10 PM.
- Tips: Arrive before sunset to enjoy the breathtaking views of the city as it transitions from day to night. The terrace is particularly lovely during the warmer months.

6. Vorderhaus (Habsburgerstraße 9, 79104 Freiburg im Breisgau, Germany)

- Overview: This vegetarian restaurant is known for its creative and delicious plant-based dishes. The cozy atmosphere and friendly service make it a popular choice for vegetarians and non-vegetarians alike.
- Menu Highlights: The menu changes seasonally, but highlights include their hearty soups, fresh salads, and innovative mains. Prices range from $15-$25 per person.
- Opening Hours: Open Monday to Saturday from 11 AM to 10 PM.
- Tips: Perfect for a healthy and satisfying meal. Their desserts are also worth trying, especially the vegan chocolate cake.

7. Schlappen (Bertoldstraße 51, 79098 Freiburg im Breisgau, Germany)

- Overview: A laid-back pub and restaurant, Schlappen is a great place to enjoy a casual meal and a drink. It's known for its lively atmosphere and eclectic menu.
- Menu Highlights: Popular dishes include their burgers, schnitzels, and the "Schlappen-Pfanne," a hearty skillet dish. Meals range from $10-$20.
- Opening Hours: Open daily from 10 AM to 2 AM.
- Tips: A great spot for nightlife as well. The pub frequently hosts live music and events, making it a fun place to hang out in the evenings.

Accommodation in Freiburg

Freiburg offers a wide range of accommodation options to suit every budget and preference. Whether you're looking for luxury, comfort, or a budget-friendly stay, you'll find something that meets your needs. Here are some top recommendations:

1. Colombi Hotel (Rotteckring 16, 79098 Freiburg im Breisgau, Germany)

- Overview: This five-star hotel offers luxurious accommodations with top-notch amenities. It's located in the heart of Freiburg, close to major attractions like the Freiburg Minster and Münsterplatz.
- Amenities: The hotel features an indoor pool, fitness center, spa, and gourmet restaurant. Rooms are elegantly furnished and offer stunning views of the city or the hotel's private park. Free Wi-Fi is available throughout the property.
- Rates: Nightly rates start at approximately $300. Address: Rotteckring 16, 79098 Freiburg im Breisgau, Germany. Website: Colombi Hotel
- Tips: Book well in advance, especially during peak tourist seasons. The hotel's in-house restaurant, Zirbelstube, is renowned for its fine dining and exceptional service.

2. Hotel Oberkirch (Münsterplatz 22, 79098 Freiburg im Breisgau, Germany)

- Overview: Located directly on Münsterplatz, this charming hotel offers a mix of traditional and modern comforts. Many rooms offer views of the Freiburg Minster, making for a memorable stay.

- Amenities: The hotel provides free Wi-Fi, a complimentary breakfast, and a cozy on-site restaurant serving regional specialties. The historic building adds to the hotel's unique charm.
- Rates: Nightly rates range from $150 to $250. Address: Münsterplatz 22, 79098 Freiburg im Breisgau, Germany. Website: Hotel Oberkirch
- Tips: Request a room with a view of the Minster for an unforgettable experience. The central location is perfect for exploring the old town on foot.

3. Hotel Barbara (Poststraße 4, 79098 Freiburg im Breisgau, Germany)

- Overview: This family-run boutique hotel is known for its warm hospitality and convenient location near the main train station and city center.
- Amenities: Guests enjoy free Wi-Fi, a hearty breakfast buffet, and comfortable, well-appointed rooms. The hotel's friendly staff is always ready to provide tips and recommendations for exploring the city.
- Rates: Nightly rates range from $100 to $180. Address: Poststraße 4, 79098 Freiburg im Breisgau, Germany. Website: Hotel Barbara
- Tips: Ideal for travelers looking for a comfortable and affordable stay. The hotel's central location makes it easy to access public transportation and major attractions.

4. Mercure Hotel Freiburg Am Münster (Auf der Zinnen 1, 79098 Freiburg im Breisgau, Germany)

- Overview: This modern hotel offers comfortable accommodations with excellent amenities, including a restaurant, bar, and meeting facilities. It's

conveniently located near the Freiburg Minster and the city's historic center.
- Amenities: The hotel features free Wi-Fi, a fitness center, and a business center. Rooms are contemporary and well-equipped, ensuring a pleasant stay.
- Rates: Nightly rates range from $120 to $200. Address: Auf der Zinnen 1, 79098 Freiburg im Breisgau, Germany. Website: Mercure Hotel Freiburg Am Münster
- Tips: Perfect for business travelers and tourists alike. The hotel's restaurant, "Munsterblick," offers a great breakfast buffet and stunning views of the Freiburg Minster.

5. Youth Hostel Freiburg (Kartäuserstraße 151, 79104 Freiburg im Breisgau, Germany)

- Overview: Ideal for budget travelers, this hostel offers clean, basic accommodations and a friendly atmosphere. It's located a bit outside the city center but is easily accessible by public transport.
- Amenities: Free Wi-Fi, breakfast included, and communal kitchen facilities. Dormitory and private rooms are available, catering to a variety of travelers.
- Rates: Dormitory beds start at $25 per night, private rooms from $50. Address: Kartäuserstraße 151, 79104 Freiburg im Breisgau, Germany. Website: Youth Hostel Freiburg
- Tips: Great option for young travelers and those on a tight budget. The hostel often organizes social activities and tours, perfect for meeting other travelers.

6. Hotel Minerva (Poststraße 8, 79098 Freiburg im Breisgau, Germany)

- Overview: This boutique hotel offers a charming stay with a touch of elegance. It's centrally located, making it easy to explore the city.
- Amenities: The hotel features free Wi-Fi, a complimentary breakfast, and comfortable rooms with unique decor. The garden terrace is a lovely spot for a morning coffee.
- Rates: Nightly rates range from $100 to $180. Address: Poststraße 8, 79098 Freiburg im Breisgau, Germany. Website: Hotel Minerva
- Tips: Ideal for couples and solo travelers looking for a quiet and charming place to stay. The staff is known for their friendly and helpful service.

7. Stadthotel Freiburg Kolping Hotels & Resorts (Karlstraße 7, 79104 Freiburg im Breisgau, Germany)

- Overview: This eco-friendly hotel offers modern accommodations with a focus on sustainability. It's located near the old town, providing easy access to Freiburg's attractions.
- Amenities: Free Wi-Fi, a restaurant serving organic meals, and well-furnished rooms. The hotel also features conference facilities for business travelers.
- Rates: Nightly rates range from $120 to $200. Address: Karlstraße 7, 79104 Freiburg im Breisgau, Germany. Website: Stadthotel Freiburg
- Tips: Ideal for environmentally conscious travelers. The hotel's commitment to sustainability is reflected in its operations and amenities.

8. Hotel Rappen (Münsterplatz 13, 79098 Freiburg im Breisgau, Germany)

- Overview: Located directly on Münsterplatz, Hotel Rappen offers comfortable accommodations with a historic touch. Many rooms provide views of the Freiburg Minster.
- Amenities: Free Wi-Fi, a complimentary breakfast, and an on-site restaurant. The hotel also offers meeting facilities for business travelers.
- Rates: Nightly rates range from $150 to $250. Address: Münsterplatz 13, 79098 Freiburg im Breisgau, Germany. Website: Hotel Rappen
- Tips: The hotel's prime location makes it an excellent choice for exploring the old town. Request a room with a Minster view for a memorable stay.

9. Hotel Hirschen (Breisgauer Straße 47, 79110 Freiburg im Breisgau, Germany)

- Overview: This four-star hotel offers a luxurious stay with modern amenities. It's located in the western part of Freiburg, offering a quieter environment.
- Amenities: The hotel features free Wi-Fi, a fitness center, spa services, and an on-site restaurant serving regional and international cuisine. The outdoor pool is a highlight during the summer months.
- Rates: Nightly rates range from $180 to $300. Address: Breisgauer Straße 47, 79110 Freiburg im Breisgau, Germany. Website: Hotel Hirschen
- Tips: Ideal for travelers looking for a more relaxed and upscale stay. The hotel's spa services are perfect for unwinding after a day of exploring.

10. Hotel Classic (Gundelfinger Straße 27B, 79108 Freiburg im Breisgau, Germany)

- Overview: A modern hotel offering comfortable accommodations at an affordable price. It's located in the northern part of Freiburg, with good public transport connections to the city center.
- Amenities: Free Wi-Fi, complimentary breakfast, and well-appointed rooms with modern amenities. The hotel also offers free parking for guests.
- Rates: Nightly rates range from $80 to $150. Address: Gundelfinger Straße 27B, 79108 Freiburg im Breisgau, Germany. Website: Hotel Classic
- Tips: Great option for travelers with a car, as the hotel offers free parking. The nearby tram stop makes it easy to reach the city center.

3.2 Baden-Baden

3.2.1 Thermal Spas

Baden-Baden is synonymous with luxury and wellness, and its thermal spas are the epitome of relaxation and rejuvenation. The town's reputation as a spa destination dates back to Roman times, and today it continues to draw visitors from around the world seeking its healing waters and serene atmosphere.

1. Caracalla Spa

Caracalla Spa is a modern oasis of relaxation that seamlessly blends ancient traditions with contemporary luxury. Named after the Roman emperor Caracalla, who was a devotee of thermal baths, this spa offers a holistic wellness experience that caters to all senses.

Thermal Pools:

The spa features a series of indoor and outdoor thermal pools, each filled with mineral-rich water sourced from the hot springs deep beneath the Black Forest. The water temperatures range from 68°F to 104°F (20°C to 40°C), allowing you to choose the perfect warmth for your relaxation. The outdoor pools, surrounded by lush greenery, are particularly enchanting, offering stunning views and a tranquil atmosphere. Underwater music and massage jets enhance the experience, melting away stress and tension.

Saunas:

Caracalla Spa's extensive sauna area is a sanctuary for sauna enthusiasts. It includes several types of saunas:

- Finnish Saunas: These traditional high-temperature saunas, maintained at around 185°F (85°C), provide an intense and purifying heat that promotes detoxification.
- Aroma Sauna: Infused with aromatic essences, this sauna offers a sensory delight, combining the therapeutic benefits of heat with the soothing effects of essential oils.
- Brine Inhalation Room: This room is designed to replicate the salty air of a sea climate, enhancing respiratory health and overall well-being.

Relaxation Rooms:

After indulging in the thermal pools and saunas, unwind in one of the spa's serene relaxation rooms. These rooms feature heated loungers, cozy corners, and calming views of the surrounding gardens. It's the perfect space to relax, read, or simply enjoy the tranquility.

Wellness Treatments:

Caracalla Spa offers a variety of wellness treatments, ensuring a personalized experience for every guest. From classic massages to specialized therapies like hot stone massages and aromatherapy, the skilled therapists provide treatments tailored to your specific needs. Prices for massages start at around $70 for a 30-minute session, with extended treatments available for deeper relaxation.

Practical Information:

- Opening Hours: Caracalla Spa is open daily from 8 a.m. to 10 p.m., with the sauna area opening at 9 a.m.
- Admission Fees: A three-hour pass costs approximately $20, while a full-day pass is around $35. Wellness treatments are priced separately.
- Address and Contact: Römerpl. 1, 76530 Baden-Baden, Germany. Website: caracalla.de

Visiting Caracalla Spa is more than just a spa day; it's an immersive experience that rejuvenates both body and mind. The variety of facilities and treatments ensures there's something for everyone, whether you're looking for a quick dip or a full day of pampering.

2. Friedrichsbad

For those seeking a more traditional experience, Friedrichsbad offers a journey back in time with its Roman-Irish bathing ritual. This historic bathhouse, built in 1877, is an architectural marvel that combines the opulence of the Roman Empire with the therapeutic practices of Irish steam baths.

Thermal Baths:

The bathing ritual at Friedrichsbad is a meticulously designed 17-step process that takes you through a series of temperature-controlled baths, steam rooms, and relaxation stages. The journey begins with a warm-air bath, followed by progressively warmer thermal pools. The highlight is the central dome pool, a grand space with a soaring stained-glass dome that bathes the room in a soft, colorful light. Floating in the warm, mineral-rich waters beneath this dome is a truly sublime experience.

Steam Rooms:

Friedrichsbad's steam rooms are infused with natural thermal steam, which helps to open pores, detoxify the skin, and promote deep relaxation. The eucalyptus-scented steam room is particularly popular, offering a refreshing and invigorating atmosphere that enhances the cleansing process.

Scrubbing Stations:

One of the unique aspects of Friedrichsbad is the soap and brush massage, a traditional scrubbing ritual that exfoliates the skin, leaving it feeling smooth and revitalized. Performed by skilled attendants, this massage uses a combination of soap lather and natural bristle brushes to cleanse and invigorate the skin. It's a key part of the bathing experience and adds to the overall sense of well-being.

Relaxation Areas:

After completing the bathing ritual, guests can relax in the tranquil rest rooms. These areas feature heated loungers, soft blankets, and a peaceful ambiance that encourages deep relaxation. The relaxation area also includes a reading room with a selection of books and magazines, perfect for unwinding after your bath.

Practical Information:

- Opening Hours: Friedrichsbad is open daily from 9 a.m. to 10 p.m., with the last admission at 8 p.m.
- Admission Fees: A full bathing experience costs approximately $45, including the soap and brush massage. Discounts are available for children and seniors.
- Address and Contact: Römerpl. 1, 76530 Baden-Baden, Germany

A visit to Friedrichsbad is a journey through history and wellness. The unique combination of Roman and Irish traditions offers a deeply relaxing experience that rejuvenates both body and soul. The detailed and structured bathing process ensures that every visitor enjoys the full benefits of the thermal waters and the serene environment.

Tips for Maximizing Your Thermal Spa Experience

To make the most of your visit to Baden-Baden's thermal spas, consider the following tips:

1. Plan Your Visit:

Decide in advance whether you want a modern spa experience at Caracalla Spa or a traditional bathing ritual at Friedrichsbad. Each offers a unique experience, and understanding the differences will help you choose the one that best suits your preferences.

2. Allocate Enough Time:

Thermal spa experiences are best enjoyed without rushing. Allocate at least three to four hours to fully immerse yourself in the treatments and facilities. A full-day pass can be particularly rewarding if you want to enjoy multiple treatments and relaxation areas.

3. Hydrate Well:

Thermal baths and saunas can be dehydrating. Drink plenty of water before, during, and after your visit to stay hydrated. Many spas provide water stations or herbal teas to help you stay refreshed.

4. Bring Essential Items:

While most spas provide towels and robes, consider bringing your own bathing suit, flip-flops, and a water bottle. If you plan to enjoy the saunas, remember that some may require nudity or specific attire, so check the spa's policies beforehand.

5. Book Treatments in Advance:

Wellness treatments like massages and facials can be highly popular. To ensure you get your desired time slot, book your treatments in advance, either online or by calling the spa.

6. Respect Spa Etiquette:

Maintain a quiet and respectful demeanor in relaxation areas to preserve the tranquil atmosphere. Follow the spa's guidelines for sauna use, such as showering before entering and using towels on sauna benches.

7. Explore Spa Packages:

Many spas offer packages that combine entry fees with treatments or meals, often at a discounted rate. These packages can provide excellent value and a more comprehensive experience.

8. Consider Off-Peak Times:

To avoid crowds and enjoy a more peaceful experience, consider visiting the spas during off-peak times. Early mornings and weekdays are typically less busy than weekends and afternoons.

3.2.2 Cultural Sites

Baden-Baden is not only a haven for wellness enthusiasts but also a cultural gem, offering a wealth of historical and artistic experiences. The town's rich cultural heritage is reflected in its museums, theaters, and historic landmarks.

1. Museum Frieder Burda

Museum Frieder Burda is a beacon of contemporary art in Baden-Baden. Situated within the scenic Lichtentaler Allee park, this museum is renowned for its striking architecture and impressive collection of modern and contemporary art.

Exhibitions and Features:

- Permanent Collection: The museum's permanent collection includes over 1,000 works of art, focusing on German Expressionism and post-war European art. Notable artists featured in the collection include Pablo Picasso, Gerhard Richter, and Jackson Pollock. The museum's dedication to German Expressionism is evident in its extensive display of works by Ernst Ludwig Kirchner and Max Beckmann, offering visitors a deep dive into this pivotal movement.
- Temporary Exhibitions: In addition to its permanent collection, Museum Frieder Burda hosts several temporary exhibitions each year. These exhibitions often highlight contemporary artists and include interactive installations and multimedia presentations. Recent exhibitions have featured artists like Neo Rauch and Katharina Grosse, whose vibrant works provide a fresh perspective on modern art.

- Architectural Highlights: Designed by the American architect Richard Meier, the museum building itself is a work of art. Meier's use of natural light and his seamless integration of indoor and outdoor spaces create a harmonious environment that enhances the viewing experience. The museum's white façade, large windows, and open spaces reflect Meier's signature style and offer a tranquil setting for art appreciation.

Practical Information:

- Opening Hours: Open Tuesday to Sunday from 10 a.m. to 6 p.m. Closed on Mondays.
- Admission Fees: General admission is around $15. Discounts are available for students, seniors, and groups.
- Address and Contact: Lichtentaler Allee 8b, 76530 Baden-Baden, Germany.

2. Staatliche Kunsthalle Baden-Baden

Adjacent to the Museum Frieder Burda, the Staatliche Kunsthalle Baden-Baden is another cultural hotspot that should not be missed. This institution, which dates back to 1909, focuses on contemporary art and plays a significant role in the cultural landscape of Baden-Baden.

Exhibitions and Features:

- Permanent and Temporary Exhibitions: The Kunsthalle does not maintain a permanent collection but instead focuses on changing exhibitions that showcase contemporary art from around the world. These exhibitions cover a wide range of mediums, including painting, sculpture, photography, and video

art. Past exhibitions have featured artists such as Marina Abramović and Olafur Eliasson.
- Public Programs: The Kunsthalle also hosts a variety of public programs, including artist talks, workshops, and lectures. These programs provide visitors with the opportunity to engage with contemporary art on a deeper level and often include interactive components that encourage audience participation.

Practical Information:

- Opening Hours: Open Tuesday to Sunday from 10 a.m. to 6 p.m. Closed on Mondays.
- Admission Fees: Admission fees vary depending on the exhibition. General admission typically ranges from $8 to $12.
- Address and Contact: Lichtentaler Allee 8a, 76530 Baden-Baden, Germany. Website: kunsthalle-baden-baden.de

3. Kurhaus and Casino Baden-Baden

The Kurhaus is one of Baden-Baden's most iconic landmarks. This magnificent building, constructed in the 19th century, serves as the town's cultural and social hub. Adjacent to the Kurhaus is the world-famous Casino Baden-Baden, known for its opulent interiors and rich history.

Highlights and Features:

- Concert Hall: The Kurhaus's concert hall is renowned for its exceptional acoustics and elegant design. It hosts performances by international orchestras, soloists, and ballet companies. The hall's grand architecture and plush seating make attending a concert here a truly memorable experience. Some

notable events include the Baden-Baden Easter Festival, featuring the Berlin Philharmonic, and the annual New Year's Concert.
- Casino: The Casino Baden-Baden, often described as the most beautiful casino in the world, offers a glamorous gaming experience. The casino features classic table games like roulette, blackjack, and poker, as well as a selection of slot machines. The opulent décor, inspired by French palaces, adds to the luxurious atmosphere. The casino's history dates back to 1824, and it has since hosted numerous celebrities and royals, adding to its allure.
- Festivals and Events: The Kurhaus is also a venue for various festivals, including the Baden-Baden Summer Nights Festival and the New Year's Eve Gala. These events attract visitors from all over the world and offer a taste of the town's vibrant cultural scene. The summer festival, held in the Kurhaus's gardens, features open-air concerts and theatrical performances.

Practical Information:

- Opening Hours: The Kurhaus is open daily, with events scheduled throughout the year. The casino is open from 2 p.m. to 2 a.m.
- Admission Fees: Concert ticket prices vary depending on the performance. Entry to the casino is around $5, with additional costs for gaming.
- Address and Contact: Kaiserallee 1, 76530 Baden-Baden, Germany. Website: kurhaus-badenbaden.de

4. Fabergé Museum

The Fabergé Museum in Baden-Baden is a unique institution dedicated to the works of the famous Russian jeweler Peter Carl Fabergé. This private museum houses the world's largest collection of Fabergé pieces, offering visitors a glimpse into the opulence of the Russian Imperial Court.

Exhibitions and Features:

- Permanent Collection: The museum's collection includes over 700 pieces, with highlights such as Fabergé eggs, jewelry, and objets d'art. The Fabergé eggs, in particular, are the museum's main attraction. These intricately designed eggs, created for the Russian tsars, are masterpieces of craftsmanship and artistry.
- Temporary Exhibitions: In addition to its permanent collection, the museum hosts temporary exhibitions that focus on various aspects of Fabergé's work and the broader context of Russian decorative arts. These exhibitions provide a deeper understanding of the historical and cultural significance of Fabergé's creations.

Practical Information:

- Opening Hours: Open daily from 10 a.m. to 6 p.m.
- Admission Fees: General admission is around $15. Discounts are available for students, seniors, and children.
- Address and Contact: Sophienstraße 30, 76530 Baden-Baden, Germany. Website: faberge-museum.de

5. Theater Baden-Baden

The Theater Baden-Baden is one of Germany's oldest and most prestigious theaters. Built in 1862, this historic venue offers a diverse program of performances, including opera, ballet, drama, and concerts.

Performances and Features:

- Opera and Ballet: The theater's opera and ballet performances are particularly renowned. The resident company, Baden-Baden Philharmonic Orchestra, performs both classical and contemporary works, attracting top talent from around the world. The theater's annual opera festival is a highlight, featuring productions of both well-known and rare operas.
- Drama: The theater also hosts a variety of dramatic productions, ranging from classic plays by Shakespeare and Goethe to contemporary works by modern playwrights. These performances often feature innovative staging and direction, making for a dynamic theater-going experience.
- Concerts: In addition to opera and drama, the theater hosts concerts by both local and international musicians. The theater's intimate setting provides an ideal atmosphere for chamber music and solo recitals.

Practical Information:

- Opening Hours: Performance times vary. Check the theater's website for the current schedule.
- Admission Fees: Ticket prices vary depending on the performance. Prices typically range from $20 to $100.
- Address and Contact: Goetheplatz 1, 76530 Baden-Baden, Germany. Phone: +49 7221 932700.

6. Brahms House

The Brahms House, located in the Lichtental district of Baden-Baden, is the former summer residence of the famous composer Johannes Brahms. This charming museum offers a glimpse into the life and work of Brahms during his time in Baden-Baden.

Exhibitions and Features:

- Historical Rooms: The house has been preserved to reflect the period when Brahms lived and worked here. Visitors can see the composer's study, where he wrote some of his most famous works, including the Symphony No. 1 and the German Requiem. The study contains original furniture, manuscripts, and personal items that belonged to Brahms.
- Guided Tours: The museum offers guided tours that provide detailed information about Brahms's life and his connection to Baden-Baden. These tours offer fascinating insights into the composer's creative process and his influence on the musical world.
- Concerts: The Brahms House also hosts intimate concerts and recitals, featuring works by Brahms and other composers of his era. These performances take place in the house's small concert hall, creating a unique and atmospheric experience.

Practical Information:

- Opening Hours: Open Tuesday to Sunday from 10 a.m. to 5 p.m. Closed on Mondays.
- Admission Fees: General admission is around $10. Discounts are available for students and seniors.
- Address and Contact: Maximilianstraße 85, 76530 Baden-Baden, Germany. Website: brahms-baden-baden.de

7. Lichtentaler Allee

Lichtentaler Allee is more than just a beautiful park; it's a cultural landmark that has been a central part of Baden-Baden's history for centuries. This picturesque avenue stretches for over two kilometers along the banks of the Oos River, offering a serene escape from the hustle and bustle of the town.

Features and Attractions:

- Historical Significance: Lichtentaler Allee has been a popular promenade since the 17th century. It has been frequented by many notable figures, including royalty, artists, and writers. Today, it remains a beloved spot for both locals and visitors.
- Botanical Diversity: The park is home to an impressive array of trees and plants, including rare species from around the world. Visitors can enjoy the sight of ancient oaks, colorful flower beds, and meticulously maintained lawns.
- Cultural Institutions: Along the avenue, you'll find several important cultural institutions, including the Museum Frieder Burda, the Staatliche Kunsthalle, and the Theater Baden-Baden. These institutions add a rich cultural dimension to the natural beauty of the park.
- Statues and Monuments: Lichtentaler Allee is dotted with statues and monuments that commemorate important figures and events in Baden-Baden's history. These include statues of Johannes Brahms and Clara Schumann, as well as memorials to local historical events.

Practical Information:

- Opening Hours: The park is open to the public year-round, with no specific opening or closing times.
- Admission Fees: Entrance to the park is free. Fees may apply for entrance to the cultural institutions located along the avenue.

3.2.3 Luxury Experiences

Baden-Baden is a destination synonymous with luxury, offering high-end experiences that cater to discerning travelers. From fine dining to upscale shopping and opulent accommodations, the town promises a lavish getaway.

Fine Dining

Baden-Baden's culinary scene is nothing short of spectacular. The town boasts several Michelin-starred restaurants, where world-class chefs create culinary masterpieces using the finest ingredients. Here are some top recommendations for an unforgettable dining experience.

1. Restaurant Le Jardin de France

Located in the heart of Baden-Baden, Restaurant Le Jardin de France offers an elegant dining experience with a French-inspired menu. This Michelin-starred restaurant is known for its exquisite dishes, impeccable service, and romantic ambiance.

Highlights and Features:

- Cuisine: The menu features a blend of traditional French cuisine with a modern twist. Signature dishes include foie gras terrine, lobster bisque, and duck breast with seasonal vegetables. The tasting menu,

which changes seasonally, is a culinary journey that showcases the chef's creativity and skill.
- Ambiance: The restaurant's interior is chic and sophisticated, with soft lighting, elegant décor, and an intimate atmosphere. During the warmer months, guests can dine on the charming outdoor terrace, surrounded by lush greenery.
- Wine Selection: The extensive wine list features a curated selection of French and international wines, perfectly paired with the dishes. The sommelier is on hand to recommend the best pairings.

Practical Information:

- Address: Lichtentaler Str. 13, 76530 Baden-Baden, Germany.
- Website: lejardindefrance.de
- Average Cost: The tasting menu is priced at approximately $150 per person.
- Opening Hours: Open Tuesday to Saturday from 6:30 p.m. to 10:30 p.m. Closed on Sunday and Monday.

2. Röttele's Restaurant & Residenz im Schloss Neuweier

For a truly unique dining experience, visit Röttele's Restaurant & Residenz im Schloss Neuweier. Set in a historic castle, this Michelin-starred restaurant offers a perfect blend of tradition and innovation.

Highlights and Features:

- Cuisine: The menu features regional and international dishes, with a focus on seasonal and locally sourced ingredients. Standout dishes include venison loin with red cabbage and juniper sauce, and turbot with champagne sauerkraut.

- Ambiance: The restaurant's setting within a castle adds to its charm and elegance. The dining rooms are adorned with antique furnishings, chandeliers, and artwork, creating a regal atmosphere.
- Wine Cellar: The castle's wine cellar boasts an impressive collection of wines, including rare vintages and local favorites. Guests can enjoy wine tastings and tours of the cellar.

Practical Information:

- Address: Mauerbergstraße 21, 76534 Baden-Baden, Germany.
- Average Cost: The three-course menu starts at around $80.
- Opening Hours: Open Wednesday to Sunday from 12 p.m. to 2:30 p.m. and 6:30 p.m. to 10 p.m. Closed on Monday and Tuesday.

Upscale Shopping

Baden-Baden's shopping scene is as refined as its culinary offerings. The town is home to a variety of luxury boutiques and specialty stores, offering everything from designer clothing to unique souvenirs. Whether you're looking to update your wardrobe or find the perfect gift, Baden-Baden's upscale shopping options will not disappoint.

1. Sophienstraße

Sophienstraße is the premier shopping street in Baden-Baden, lined with high-end boutiques and jewelers. This elegant street is a shopper's paradise, offering the latest fashion trends and timeless classics.

Notable Shops:

- Hermès: This iconic French brand offers a range of luxury goods, including scarves, handbags, and ready-to-wear clothing. The Hermès store in Baden-Baden is known for its personalized service and exclusive collections.
- Louis Vuitton: Another renowned luxury brand, Louis Vuitton offers an exquisite selection of leather goods, accessories, and clothing. The store's chic interior and attentive staff make shopping here a pleasure.
- Bucherer: For fine jewelry and watches, visit Bucherer. This prestigious store offers a curated selection of pieces from brands like Rolex, Cartier, and Chopard. Whether you're looking for a statement piece or a timeless classic, Bucherer has something for every taste.

2. Gernsbacher Straße

Gernsbacher Straße is another popular shopping area, offering a mix of luxury boutiques and charming local shops. This pedestrian-friendly street is perfect for a leisurely shopping experience.

Notable Shops:

- Juwelier Spinner: This family-owned jeweler offers a selection of fine jewelry and watches, including custom designs and bespoke pieces. The store's friendly staff and personalized service make it a favorite among locals and visitors alike.

- **Modehaus Zinser:** For high-end fashion, visit Modehaus Zinser. This multi-brand store offers a curated selection of clothing and accessories from designers like Hugo Boss, Max Mara, and Marc Cain.
- **Schuhhaus Klauser:** This upscale shoe store offers a range of stylish and comfortable footwear for men and women. From designer heels to casual sneakers, Schuhhaus Klauser has something for every occasion.

Opulent Accommodations

Baden-Baden's accommodations are as luxurious as its dining and shopping options. The town offers a range of opulent hotels, each providing exceptional service and world-class amenities. Here are some top recommendations for an unforgettable stay.

1. Brenners Park-Hotel & Spa

Brenners Park-Hotel & Spa is an iconic hotel set in a private park along the Lichtentaler Allee. This grand hotel epitomizes luxury, offering spacious rooms and suites, a state-of-the-art spa, and gourmet dining.

Highlights and Features:

- **Rooms and Suites:** The hotel's rooms and suites are elegantly decorated, featuring plush furnishings, marble bathrooms, and stunning views of the park or the town. Each room is equipped with modern amenities, including flat-screen TVs, minibars, and complimentary Wi-Fi.
- **Spa and Wellness:** The Brenners Spa offers a range of treatments, from massages and facials to hydrotherapy and aromatherapy. The spa features an

indoor pool, saunas, and a fitness center, providing a sanctuary of relaxation and rejuvenation.
- Dining: The hotel's restaurant, Fritz & Felix, offers a modern dining experience with a focus on seasonal and locally sourced ingredients. The menu features a mix of international and regional dishes, expertly prepared by the hotel's talented chefs.
- Additional Amenities: Brenners Park-Hotel & Spa also offers a range of additional amenities, including a concierge service, valet parking, and a business center. The hotel's attentive staff ensures that every guest's needs are met.

Practical Information:

- Address: Schillerstraße 4/6, 76530 Baden-Baden, Germany.
- Website: brenners.com
- Average Cost: Room rates start at approximately $400 per night.
- Check-in/Check-out: Check-in is from 3 p.m., and check-out is until 12 p.m.

2. Hotel Belle Epoque

Hotel Belle Epoque is housed in a beautiful 19th-century villa, offering a charming and luxurious stay. This boutique hotel features elegantly decorated rooms, a serene garden, and afternoon tea service.

Highlights and Features:

- Rooms: Each room at Hotel Belle Epoque is uniquely decorated, featuring antique furnishings, rich fabrics, and modern amenities. Guests can choose from a

variety of room types, including deluxe rooms and suites.
- Garden: The hotel's garden is a tranquil oasis, perfect for relaxing with a book or enjoying a leisurely stroll. During the summer months, guests can enjoy breakfast or afternoon tea in the garden.
- Afternoon Tea: Hotel Belle Epoque offers a traditional afternoon tea service, featuring a selection of teas, finger sandwiches, scones, and pastries. This delightful experience is a highlight for many guests.
- Additional Amenities: The hotel offers a range of additional amenities, including complimentary Wi-Fi, a concierge service, and airport transfers. The friendly and attentive staff are always on hand to assist with any requests.

Practical Information:

- Address: Maria-Viktoria-Str. 2c, 76530 Baden-Baden, Germany.
- Website: hotel-belle-epoque.de
- Average Cost: Rates start at around $250 per night.
- Check-in/Check-out: Check-in is from 2 p.m., and check-out is until 11 a.m.

Exclusive Events and Festivals

Baden-Baden is renowned for its exclusive events and festivals, which attract visitors from around the world. These events offer a taste of the town's vibrant cultural scene and provide an opportunity to experience its elegance and charm.

1. Baden-Baden Summer Nights Festival

Held annually in July, the Baden-Baden Summer Nights Festival is a celebration of music, dance, and theater. The festival takes place in the stunning setting of the Kurpark, with performances held in the open-air pavilion and throughout the park.

Highlights and Features:

- Concerts: The festival features a diverse lineup of concerts, including classical music, jazz, and contemporary performances. Renowned orchestras, soloists, and bands perform against the backdrop of the beautiful park.
- Dance and Theater: In addition to music, the festival includes dance and theater performances. Guests can enjoy ballet, modern dance, and theatrical productions by talented artists from around the world.
- Gourmet Food and Wine: The festival also offers a range of gourmet food and wine options, with pop-up restaurants and bars serving delicious dishes and fine wines. It's the perfect opportunity to sample local and international cuisine in a festive setting.

Practical Information:

- Dates: The festival typically takes place in the last two weeks of July. Exact dates and the program are announced on the festival's website.
- Tickets: Ticket prices vary depending on the performance. It's advisable to book in advance, as popular events can sell out quickly.

2. New Year's Eve Gala

Ring in the New Year in style at the Baden-Baden New Year's Eve Gala, held at the historic Kurhaus. This glamorous event is one of the highlights of the town's social calendar, offering a night of music, dancing, and celebration.

Highlights and Features:

- Gala Dinner: The evening begins with a sumptuous gala dinner, featuring a multi-course menu prepared by top chefs. Guests can enjoy gourmet dishes paired with fine wines and champagne.
- Live Music and Dancing: After dinner, the ballroom comes alive with live music and dancing. A live band performs a mix of classic and contemporary hits, ensuring a lively and festive atmosphere.
- Midnight Celebration: As the clock strikes midnight, guests gather to toast the New Year with champagne. The celebration continues with more music and dancing into the early hours of the morning.

Practical Information:

- Date and Time: The New Year's Eve Gala is held on December 31, with festivities starting at 7 p.m. and continuing until 2 a.m.
- Tickets: Tickets for the gala dinner and celebration are priced at approximately $300 per person. It's advisable to book early, as this popular event often sells out.
- Address: Kaiserallee 1, 76530 Baden-Baden, Germany.

Baden-Baden's blend of fine dining, upscale shopping, opulent accommodations, and exclusive events makes it a standout destination for luxury travelers.

3.3 Triberg

Nestled in the heart of the Black Forest, Triberg is a picturesque town renowned for its natural beauty and rich cultural heritage. Visitors are drawn to Triberg for its stunning waterfalls, world-famous cuckoo clocks, and delectable local cuisine. Here's an in-depth look at what makes Triberg a must-visit destination in the Black Forest.

3.3.1 Waterfalls

Triberg Waterfalls are one of the most iconic natural attractions in the Black Forest, drawing visitors from around the world to experience their beauty and grandeur. Standing as Germany's highest waterfalls, they offer a dramatic cascade over seven steps, dropping a total of 163 meters (535 feet). These waterfalls are not just a natural spectacle; they are an integral part of Triberg's charm and a must-see for any visitor to the region.

Getting to the Waterfalls

Triberg is conveniently located in the heart of the Black Forest, making it accessible from various major cities. The waterfalls are situated at Hauptstraße 85, 78098 Triberg, just a short walk from the town center.

- By Car: If you're driving, follow the well-marked signs to Triberg from the B33 highway. There are several parking lots near the entrance of the waterfalls, including one directly at the Hauptstraße entrance. Parking fees are around $3 for a full day.
- By Train: The Deutsche Bahn offers regular services to Triberg. From the train station, it's a 15-minute walk

to the waterfalls. Alternatively, local buses and taxis are available.
- **By Bus:** Buses connect Triberg with nearby towns and cities. Check the local bus schedules for the most convenient routes.

Admission and Opening Hours

The Triberg Waterfalls are open year-round, offering different experiences in each season. The falls are particularly impressive during spring and summer when the water flow is at its peak due to snowmelt and rainfall.

Opening Hours:

- Summer (April to October): Daily from 9:00 AM to 6:00 PM.
- Winter (November to March): Daily from 10:00 AM to 5:00 PM.

Admission Fees:

- Adults: $6
- Children (6-15): $4
- Family Ticket (2 adults + 2 children): $15

Exploring the Waterfalls

The Triberg Waterfalls are situated within the Black Forest Nature Park, a protected area that preserves the natural beauty and biodiversity of the region. Three main trails cater to different fitness levels and interests, ensuring that every visitor can enjoy the falls to the fullest.

1. Lower Trail:

- Difficulty: Easy
- Distance: 0.5 miles

- Duration: 30 minutes to 1 hour

Description: The Lower Trail is perfect for families with young children and those with limited mobility. It features a gentle incline and several well-maintained viewing platforms that offer excellent photo opportunities. Interpretive signs along the trail provide information about the local flora and fauna, adding an educational element to the visit.

2. Middle Trail:

- Difficulty: Moderate
- Distance: 1 mile
- Duration: 1 to 1.5 hours

Description: This trail takes you closer to the cascading waters and through lush forested areas. It's an excellent choice for those looking to immerse themselves in nature while enjoying the scenic views of the falls. The path is well-marked and includes several bridges that cross over the streams, providing different angles of the waterfalls.

3. Upper Trail:

- Difficulty: Challenging
- Distance: 2 miles
- Duration: 2 to 3 hours

Description: For the more adventurous, the Upper Trail offers a steeper climb and rocky paths, but the effort is well worth it. This trail leads you to the top of the waterfalls, where panoramic views of the surrounding Black Forest await. The tranquility and beauty of the upper cascades are a reward for the challenging hike.

Best Times to Visit

While the Triberg Waterfalls are spectacular year-round, each season offers a unique perspective.

- Spring: Melting snow and increased rainfall make spring an ideal time to visit, with the waterfalls at their most powerful. The surrounding forest comes to life with blossoming flowers and fresh greenery.
- Summer: Warm weather and long days provide perfect conditions for hiking and picnicking. The waterfalls are a popular spot, so visiting early in the morning or late in the afternoon can help avoid crowds.
- Autumn: The fall foliage adds a stunning backdrop to the waterfalls, making it a favorite time for photographers. Cooler temperatures make hiking comfortable, and the trails are less crowded.
- Winter: Partially frozen waterfalls create a magical, icy landscape. The trails can be slippery, so proper footwear and caution are necessary. Winter is the quietest season, offering a peaceful and serene experience.

Amenities and Nearby Attractions

The entrance area to the Triberg Waterfalls is equipped with several amenities to enhance your visit.

- Visitor Center: Provides maps, trail information, and answers to any questions you may have.
- Restrooms: Clean and well-maintained facilities are available near the entrance.
- Café: A cozy spot to grab a coffee or a light snack before or after your hike. During the summer months, outdoor seating allows you to enjoy the fresh air and beautiful surroundings.

- Souvenir Shop: Offers a range of local products, including postcards, maps, and traditional Black Forest crafts.

Nearby Attractions:

- Black Forest Museum: Located at Wallfahrtstraße 4, 78098 Triberg, the museum offers exhibits on local history, culture, and traditions, including an impressive collection of cuckoo clocks. Admission is $5 for adults and $3 for children.
- Maria in der Tanne: A beautiful baroque church located a short walk from the waterfalls. It's a peaceful place to reflect and admire the intricate architecture.
- Triberg Cuckoo Clock Shops: Triberg is famous for its cuckoo clocks. Shops like the House of 1000 Clocks and Oli's Schnitzstube offer a wide variety of these handcrafted timepieces.

Tips for Visiting

- Early Morning or Late Afternoon Visits: To enjoy a more peaceful experience and avoid the busiest times, plan your visit early in the morning or late in the afternoon. This timing also provides the best lighting for photography.
- Proper Footwear: The trails around the waterfalls can be uneven and slippery, especially after rain or in winter. Sturdy, comfortable hiking shoes are a must.
- Weather Preparedness: The weather in the Black Forest can change quickly. Bring a rain jacket and dress in layers to adjust to varying conditions.
- Picnic Spots: Bring a picnic and take advantage of the designated areas along the trails. Enjoying a meal

with the sound of cascading water in the background is a memorable experience.
- Photography Tips: Bring a tripod for long exposure shots to capture the silky flow of the water. Early morning and late afternoon light provide the best conditions for photography.
- Wildlife Watching: The Black Forest is home to diverse wildlife, including red deer, foxes, and a variety of bird species. Keep an eye out for these creatures, especially if you visit during the quieter times of the day.

3.3.2 Cuckoo Clocks

Triberg is synonymous with the Black Forest cuckoo clock, a symbol of German craftsmanship and tradition. The town boasts several workshops and museums dedicated to these intricate timepieces.

The History of Cuckoo Clocks

The tradition of making cuckoo clocks dates back to the early 18th century. It is believed that the first cuckoo clocks were created by Franz Anton Ketterer, a clockmaker from the village of Schönwald, near Triberg. Inspired by the bellows of church organs, Ketterer designed a mechanism that mimicked the call of the cuckoo bird.

Over the centuries, cuckoo clocks evolved, incorporating more intricate designs and mechanisms. The Black Forest became synonymous with these clocks due to the high quality of craftsmanship and the unique designs that were often inspired by local folklore and nature.

The Art of Cuckoo Clock Making

Cuckoo clocks are typically made of linden wood, which is known for its fine grain and ease of carving. The clock faces are often adorned with intricate carvings of leaves, animals, and scenes from Black Forest life. The internal mechanisms are just as impressive, featuring precision engineering that ensures the clocks keep accurate time and produce the distinctive cuckoo call on the hour.

- The clocks can be broadly categorized into two styles:
- Traditional: These clocks feature classic designs with intricate wood carvings, often depicting themes like hunting, nature, and village life.
- Chalet: Inspired by the architecture of Black Forest chalets, these clocks are detailed miniature versions of traditional houses, complete with tiny figures that dance or move when the clock strikes.

Must-Visit Cuckoo Clock Shops in Triberg

Triberg is home to several renowned cuckoo clock shops and workshops, each offering a unique glimpse into the world of clock making.

1. House of 1000 Clocks

Located at Hauptstraße 79-81, the House of 1000 Clocks is a must-visit for anyone interested in these timepieces. This extensive shop and museum display a vast collection of cuckoo clocks, from traditional designs to modern interpretations.

Opening Hours: Monday to Saturday, 9:00 AM to 7:00 PM; Sunday, 10:00 AM to 6:00 PM.

Admission: Free, but purchasing a clock can range from $50 for a simple model to several thousand dollars for elaborate pieces.

The House of 1000 Clocks not only showcases a wide variety of clocks but also provides insight into the history and craftsmanship behind them. Visitors can watch demonstrations of clock making and even see some of the artisans at work. The staff here are knowledgeable and can help you choose a clock that fits your style and budget.

2. Eble Uhren-Park

A short drive from the town center, at Schonachbach 27, Eble Uhren-Park is home to the world's largest cuckoo clock. This giant timepiece, with a 15-foot-high cuckoo, is a marvel of engineering and a fun photo spot.

Opening Hours: Daily from 9:00 AM to 6:00 PM.

Admission: Free to view the exterior, guided tours inside the clock cost $5 per person.

Eble Uhren-Park offers guided tours that provide a behind-the-scenes look at the clock's inner workings. The tour is both educational and entertaining, making it a great activity for families. After the tour, visitors can browse a large selection of cuckoo clocks in the adjacent shop, which features everything from traditional designs to contemporary pieces.

3. Oli's Schnitzstube

Located at Wallfahrtsstraße 13, Oli's Schnitzstube is a small, family-run workshop that specializes in hand-carved cuckoo clocks. Each clock is a unique piece, reflecting the individual artistry of the carver.

Opening Hours: Monday to Friday, 10:00 AM to 6:00 PM.

Admission: Free.

At Oli's Schnitzstube, you can meet the artisans and watch them at work. This intimate setting allows for a deeper appreciation of the craftsmanship that goes into each clock. The workshop also offers custom-made clocks, allowing you to commission a piece that is truly one-of-a-kind.

Choosing the Perfect Cuckoo Clock

When selecting a cuckoo clock, there are several factors to consider:

1. Authenticity

Ensure that the clock is made in the Black Forest. Authentic clocks will often come with a VdS certificate (Verein die Schwarzwalduhr), which guarantees that the clock was made in the region and meets high standards of craftsmanship.

2. Mechanism

Cuckoo clocks come with either mechanical or quartz movements. Mechanical clocks need to be wound daily or weekly, depending on the model, and are prized for their traditional engineering. Quartz clocks, on the other hand, are battery-operated and require less maintenance.

2. Design

Choose a design that resonates with you. Traditional clocks feature classic Black Forest themes, while chalet clocks depict charming house scenes. There are also modern designs for those looking for something a bit different.

4. Size and Placement

Consider where you will place the clock in your home. Measure the space to ensure the clock will fit comfortably. Also, think about the sound; some clocks have volume controls or night shut-off features to prevent the cuckoo call from disturbing your sleep.

Tips for Buying and Shipping

1. Budget

Cuckoo clocks vary widely in price, from around $50 for simple models to several thousand dollars for elaborate, hand-carved pieces. Determine your budget beforehand and discuss it with the shop staff, who can help you find a clock that fits your needs.

2. Shipping

Many shops in Triberg offer international shipping, ensuring your clock arrives safely at your home. Inquire about shipping costs and insurance to protect your purchase during transit. It's also a good idea to ask for detailed instructions on setting up and maintaining your clock once it arrives.

3. Warranty

Check if the clock comes with a warranty. Reputable shops will offer warranties that cover the clock's movement and workmanship for a certain period. This gives you peace of mind knowing that your investment is protected.

Enjoying Your Cuckoo Clock

Once you've chosen your perfect cuckoo clock, there are a few steps to ensure it functions properly and remains in excellent condition:

1. Setup

Follow the setup instructions carefully. Mechanical clocks will need to be hung on a sturdy wall and positioned correctly to ensure they run smoothly. Quartz clocks require fresh batteries, and it's important to set the time accurately.

2. Maintenance

Mechanical clocks need regular winding and occasional oiling to keep the gears running smoothly. Quartz clocks require battery changes and occasional dusting. If you're unsure about maintenance, many shops offer services to help you care for your clock.

3. Display

Choose a prominent spot to display your clock, where it can be appreciated by everyone. Ensure it is placed away from direct sunlight and moisture, which can damage the wood and mechanisms.

3.3.3 Local Cuisine

Triberg offers a taste of traditional Black Forest cuisine, characterized by hearty dishes and fresh, locally sourced ingredients. Dining in Triberg is a delightful experience, with numerous restaurants and cafés providing a warm and welcoming atmosphere.

Cafe Schäfer:

Located at Hauptstraße 19, 78098 Triberg, Cafe Schäfer is famous for its Black Forest cake, or Schwarzwälder Kirschtorte. This iconic dessert, made with layers of chocolate sponge cake, cherries, and whipped cream, is a must-try.

- Opening Hours: Daily from 10:00 AM to 6:00 PM.

- Average Cost: A slice of Black Forest cake costs around $4, and a full cake is approximately $30.

Restaurant Berghuesli:

For a taste of traditional German fare, head to Restaurant Berghuesli at Obere Bahnhofstraße 20, 78098 Triberg. This cozy restaurant offers a variety of regional specialties, including schnitzel, bratwurst, and spätzle.

- Opening Hours: Tuesday to Sunday, 11:30 AM to 9:00 PM.
- Average Cost: Main courses range from $15 to $25.

Gasthaus zum Park:

Situated near the waterfalls at Gartenstraße 24, 78098 Triberg, Gasthaus zum Park provides a perfect spot for a meal after a hike. The menu features hearty Black Forest dishes like venison stew and Maultaschen (Swabian ravioli).

- Opening Hours: Daily from 11:00 AM to 10:00 PM.
- Average Cost: Expect to pay $20 for a main course.

Tips for Enjoying Local Cuisine:

- Reservations: It's advisable to book a table in advance, especially during peak tourist seasons.
- Seasonal Specials: Try seasonal dishes like white asparagus in spring or game in autumn.
- Local Beverages: Pair your meal with a local beer or a glass of Black Forest wine. Kirschwasser, a cherry brandy, is a traditional digestif worth sampling.

Triberg, with its enchanting waterfalls, iconic cuckoo clocks, and delectable cuisine, offers a quintessential Black Forest experience. Whether you're exploring the natural beauty, diving into the local culture, or savoring the culinary delights, this charming town has something to captivate every traveler.

3.4 Titisee-Neustadt

Titisee-Neustadt, a charming town in the southern Black Forest, is a favorite destination for travelers seeking natural beauty and a variety of outdoor activities. The town is divided into two main parts: Titisee, known for its beautiful lake, and Neustadt, which offers cultural attractions and traditional Black Forest experiences.

3.4.1 Lake Titisee

Lake Titisee, nestled in the heart of the southern Black Forest, is a jewel of natural beauty and a hub of activity for visitors of all ages. Surrounded by dense, dark forests and rolling hills, the lake's crystal-clear waters reflect the stunning landscapes that make this region one of Germany's most popular tourist destinations. Here, we explore the various aspects of Lake Titisee, from its scenic boat tours and invigorating swimming spots to its picturesque hiking trails and delightful dining experiences.

Activities on Lake Titisee

1 Boat Tours and Rentals

One of the most enchanting ways to experience Lake Titisee is from the water itself. Boat tours and rentals are a quintessential part of any visit, offering a unique perspective of the lake and its surroundings.

- Tourist Information: Seestraße 37, 79822 Titisee-Neustadt, +49 7652 1206, titisee.de

- Average Cost: Boat tours cost around $10 per person for a 25-minute tour, and pedal boats or rowboats can be rented for approximately $15 per hour.

Getting the Most Out of Your Boat Tour:

To fully appreciate the tranquility and beauty of Lake Titisee, take an early morning boat tour. The calm waters and morning mist create a serene atmosphere, perfect for photography and quiet reflection. Most boat tours depart from the main pier in Titisee, where you can also find various rental options for pedal boats, rowboats, and even electric boats.

For those who prefer a more active experience, renting a pedal boat or rowboat allows you to explore the lake at your own pace. Pack a small picnic and head to the center of the lake, where you can enjoy a meal surrounded by the stunning Black Forest scenery. The lake is relatively small, so even novice boaters can navigate its waters with ease.

2. Swimming

During the warmer months, Lake Titisee becomes a popular spot for swimming. The Strandbad Titisee, a lakeside beach area, offers excellent facilities for a day of sunbathing and swimming.

- Address: Strandbadstraße 9, 79822 Titisee-Neustadt
- Opening Times: Daily from 10 AM to 6 PM (May to September)
- Average Cost: Entry fee is about $5 for adults and $3 for children.

Tips for Enjoying the Strandbad Titisee:

Arrive early to secure a good spot on the grassy area or the small sandy beach. The Strandbad offers changing rooms, showers, and a café, making it convenient to spend a full day here. The water is clean and inviting, with shallow areas perfect for children to splash around safely. For those looking for a bit more adventure, there are diving platforms and designated areas for swimming laps.

3. Hiking

The area around Lake Titisee is crisscrossed with numerous hiking trails that offer breathtaking views and varying levels of difficulty. Hiking is one of the best ways to immerse yourself in the natural beauty of the Black Forest.

Popular Trails:

1. Seerundweg: This 8-kilometer loop trail circles the lake, offering a relatively easy hike suitable for all ages.

Tip: Start your hike from the town center and follow the well-marked paths. Bring a picnic and enjoy it at one of the scenic spots along the way. The trail is mostly flat, making it accessible for families and casual hikers.

2. Hochfirst Mountain: For those seeking a more challenging hike, the trail to the summit of Hochfirst offers breathtaking panoramic views of the Black Forest and, on clear days, the Swiss Alps.

- Trailhead: Begin from the Neustadt train station.
- Duration: Approximately 3 hours round trip.
- Average Cost: Free.

Tip: Bring a camera to capture the stunning vistas, especially during sunrise or sunset. The trail is steep in parts, so wear sturdy hiking boots and bring plenty of water.

Dining by the Lake

Lake Titisee is not only a haven for outdoor activities but also a place where you can indulge in delicious local cuisine. The lakeside promenade is lined with cafes and restaurants offering a variety of dining options.

Notable Dining Spots:

1. Café Becker: Known for its delicious Black Forest cake and stunning lake views.

- Address: Seestraße 6, 79822 Titisee-Neustadt
- Average Cost: A slice of Black Forest cake costs around $5.
- Tip: Visit during mid-afternoon when the café is less crowded, and you can enjoy a leisurely coffee and dessert on the terrace.

2. Bootshaus Titisee: This lakeside restaurant offers a variety of German and international dishes.

- Address: Seestraße 27, 79822 Titisee-Neustadt
- Average Cost: Main courses range from $15 to $30.
- Tip: Reserve a table in advance, especially for dinner, to secure a spot with the best view of the lake. The outdoor seating area is particularly pleasant during warm evenings.

Shopping

Lake Titisee's promenade is also a great place for shopping. Souvenir shops and boutiques offer a range of local products and handcrafted items.

Souvenir Shops:

1. Traditional Souvenirs: Numerous shops along Seestraße sell traditional Black Forest souvenirs, including cuckoo clocks, handcrafted goods, and local delicacies.

Tip: Look for shops that display "Handmade in the Black Forest" certificates to ensure you're buying authentic products. Popular items include Schwarzwälder Kirschtorte (Black Forest Cherry Cake), local honey, and artisan wood carvings.

2. Handcrafted Goods: The Black Forest is famous for its high-quality handcrafted items, from intricate cuckoo clocks to beautifully made pottery and textiles.

Tip: Visit the workshops where these items are made to see the craftsmanship firsthand and perhaps purchase a unique, personalized souvenir.

Accommodation

Whether you're looking for a luxurious stay or a cozy, budget-friendly option, Lake Titisee has a range of accommodations to suit every traveler.

Top Recommendations:

1. Maritim TitiseeHotel:

- Address: Seestraße 16, 79822 Titisee-Neustadt
- Amenities: This four-star hotel offers comfortable rooms with lake views, an indoor pool, a spa, and direct access to the lake.

- Average Cost: Rooms start at around $150 per night.
- Tip: Book a room with a balcony for a spectacular view of the sunrise over the lake.

2. Boutique Hotel Alemannenhof:

- Address: Bruderhalde 21, 79822 Titisee-Neustadt
- Amenities: A charming boutique hotel featuring traditionally decorated rooms, a restaurant serving local cuisine, and a lakeside terrace.
- Average Cost: Rooms start at around $120 per night.
- Tip: The hotel offers complimentary shuttle service to and from the train station, making it easy to get around without a car.

Wellness and Relaxation

For those seeking relaxation, Lake Titisee offers several wellness and spa options. The serene environment of the Black Forest provides the perfect backdrop for unwinding and rejuvenating.

1. Badeparadies Schwarzwald:

- Overview: This large water park features numerous pools, water slides, and wellness areas.
- Address: Am Badeparadies 1, 79822 Titisee-Neustadt, +49 7652 99790, badeparadies-schwarzwald.de
- Opening Times: Daily from 9 AM to 10 PM.
- Average Cost: Entry fees range from $20 to $30 for adults, and $15 to $25 for children, depending on the package.
- Tip: Arrive early to secure a good spot and avoid the afternoon rush. Bring your own towels to save on rental fees. The "Palmenoase" section is particularly

relaxing with its tropical plants and tranquil ambiance.

2. Spa Treatments:

Many hotels and wellness centers around Lake Titisee offer spa treatments, from traditional massages to modern therapies.

Tip: Book your treatments in advance, especially during peak seasons, to ensure availability. Some popular treatments include the Black Forest honey massage and herbal saunas.

Local Events and Festivals

Throughout the year, Lake Titisee hosts a variety of events and festivals that offer a glimpse into local culture and traditions.

Notable Events:

1. Titisee Wine Festival: Held annually in August, this festival celebrates local wines with tastings, music, and food stalls.

Tip: Visit in the evening when the atmosphere is lively, and the live music performances add to the festive mood.

2. Christmas Market: The Titisee Christmas Market, held in December, transforms the lakeside promenade into a winter wonderland with festive stalls, local crafts, and holiday treats.

Tip: Enjoy a cup of Glühwein (mulled wine) and try the local sausages and pastries while browsing for unique Christmas gifts.

Practical Information

To make the most of your visit to Lake Titisee, consider the following practical tips and information:

- Language: While German is the official language, many people in the tourist areas speak English. Learning a few basic German phrases can enhance your experience.
- Currency: The currency used is the Euro (€). ATMs are widely available, and most places accept credit cards.
- Getting Around: The KONUS Card, provided by many hotels, allows free travel on public transport throughout the Black Forest region, making it easy to explore without a car.
- Accessibility: Lake Titisee and its surrounding areas are generally accessible to visitors with mobility issues, with many paths and facilities designed to accommodate wheelchairs and strollers.

3.4.2 Outdoor Activities

Titisee-Neustadt is an outdoor enthusiast's dream. The region offers a plethora of activities, ensuring that visitors of all ages and skill levels can find something exciting to do.

Hiking and Walking Trails

1. Hochfirst Mountain:

Hochfirst Mountain is a must-visit for hiking enthusiasts. Standing at 1,192 meters, it is the highest peak in the Black Forest, offering stunning panoramic views that stretch to the Swiss Alps on clear days.

- Trailhead: Begin your hike from the Neustadt train station. Follow the well-marked trail that leads through dense forests and picturesque landscapes.
- Duration: The round trip to the summit and back takes approximately 3 hours.
- Difficulty Level: Moderate. The trail involves some steep sections but is manageable for most hikers with a moderate fitness level.
- Average Cost: Free.

Tips:

- Start early in the morning to enjoy the tranquility and catch the sunrise from the summit.
- Bring a camera to capture the breathtaking views and wear sturdy hiking boots for a comfortable trek.

2. Wutach Gorge:

For those seeking a more challenging hike, the Wutach Gorge offers rugged terrain and dramatic landscapes that are sure to impress. This deep and narrow gorge is carved by the Wutach River, providing hikers with a unique and adventurous experience.

- Trailhead: The hike can start from various points, but a popular starting place is the Schattenmühle. Shuttle services are available from Neustadt.
- Duration: Full-day hike (about 13 kilometers one way).
- Difficulty Level: Challenging. The trail includes steep climbs, narrow paths, and requires good physical condition.
- Average Cost: Free.

Tips:

- Wear sturdy hiking boots with good grip and bring plenty of water and snacks, as there are few facilities along the trail.
- Check the weather forecast before heading out, as the trail can be slippery after rain.

Cycling

Cycling in Titisee-Neustadt is a delightful way to explore the scenic beauty of the Black Forest. The region offers numerous cycling routes that range from leisurely rides to challenging mountain bike trails.

1. Titisee-Feldberg Loop:

This 40-kilometer cycling route takes you through beautiful countryside, charming villages, and offers magnificent views of the Black Forest.

- Route: Start from Titisee and follow the signs towards Feldberg. The loop brings you back to your starting point, passing through picturesque landscapes.
- Difficulty Level: Moderate. Suitable for cyclists with a reasonable level of fitness.
- Bike Rentals: Available at Drubba Rentals, Seestraße 33, 79822 Titisee-Neustadt.
- Average Cost: Bike rentals cost around $20 per day.

Tips:

- Start your ride early to avoid the midday heat and take breaks in the small villages for refreshments and local snacks.
- Wear a helmet for safety and carry a map or GPS device to stay on track.

2. Bähnle Radweg:

This family-friendly cycling path follows an old railway line, making it flat and easy for riders of all ages. It offers beautiful views and a relaxing ride through the countryside.

- Route: The path starts in Bonndorf and ends in Lenzkirch, passing through lush meadows and forests.
- Difficulty Level: Easy. Ideal for families and beginners.
- Bike Rentals: Available in nearby towns.
- Average Cost: Bike rentals cost around $15 per day.

Tips:

- Pack a picnic and enjoy it at one of the scenic spots along the route.
- Stop at the old train stations along the path to learn about the history of the railway.

Water Sports

Lake Titisee, with its clear, calm waters, is perfect for a variety of water sports. Whether you enjoy swimming, boating, or fishing, the lake offers something for everyone.

1. Swimming:

The Strandbad Titisee is a popular spot for swimming, with a sandy beach area, clean waters, and facilities for visitors.

- Address: Strandbadstraße 9, 79822 Titisee-Neustadt
- Opening Times: Daily from 10 AM to 6 PM (May to September)
- Average Cost: Entry fee is about $5 for adults and $3 for children.

Tips:

- Arrive early to secure a good spot on the beach and bring sunscreen to protect yourself from the sun.
- The beach has lifeguards on duty, making it a safe option for families with children.

2. Boat Tours and Rentals:

Exploring Lake Titisee by boat is a relaxing and scenic way to enjoy the natural beauty of the area. Options include guided boat tours or renting a boat for personal use.

- Tourist Information: Seestraße 37, 79822 Titisee-Neustadt.
- Average Cost: Boat tours cost around $10 per person for a 25-minute tour. Pedal boats or rowboats can be rented for approximately $15 per hour.

Tips:

- Take an early morning boat tour to avoid the crowds and experience the tranquil beauty of the lake as the sun rises.
- If renting a boat, bring a hat and sunglasses to protect yourself from the sun, and pack a light snack to enjoy on the water.

Winter Sports

When winter blankets the Black Forest in snow, Titisee-Neustadt transforms into a winter sports paradise. From skiing to snowshoeing, there are plenty of activities to keep you entertained during the colder months.

1. Skiing at Feldberg:

Feldberg is the highest peak in the Black Forest and offers excellent skiing opportunities for all skill levels. The ski resort features a variety of slopes, from beginner-friendly runs to challenging trails for advanced skiers.

- Ski Pass: Day passes cost around $40 for adults and $25 for children.
- Rentals: Ski equipment can be rented at Sporthaus Hirt, Passhöhe 13, 79868 Feldberg.

Tips:

- Purchase your ski pass online to save time and take advantage of early-bird discounts.
- Dress in layers to stay warm and comfortable throughout the day. Don't forget to bring gloves and a hat.

2. Snowshoeing:

Snowshoeing is a fantastic way to explore the winter wonderland of the Black Forest at a leisurely pace. Guided tours are available and provide an excellent introduction to the sport.

- Tours: Offered by Black Forest Tours, +49 7652 9197.
- Average Cost: Guided tours cost approximately $50 per person.

Tips:

- Dress in warm, waterproof clothing and wear sturdy, insulated boots.
- Bring a thermos of hot tea or cocoa to enjoy during a break and keep yourself energized.

3. Tobogganing:

For a fun-filled family activity, try tobogganing down the snowy slopes. The region offers several toboggan runs that promise excitement for all ages.

- Hochfirstschanze Toboggan Run: This historic ski jump area now offers a thrilling toboggan run.
- Average Cost: Free if you bring your own sled, or rent one for about $10 per day.

Tips:

- Ensure that children are supervised at all times, and check that the toboggan run is open and safe to use before heading out.
- Wear waterproof clothing to stay dry and warm.

Adventure Activities

For those seeking a bit more adrenaline, Titisee-Neustadt has several adventure activities that are sure to get your heart racing.

1. Action Forest Kletterwald:

This adventure park offers various climbing and zip-lining courses for different age groups and skill levels. It's a perfect place for families and groups to enjoy a day of excitement and challenge.

- Address: Strandbadstraße 3, 79822 Titisee-Neustadt.
- Opening Times: Daily from 9 AM to 6 PM (April to October).
- Average Cost: Entry fees range from $15 to $30, depending on the course.

Tips:

- Wear comfortable athletic clothing and closed-toe shoes. Ensure children are supervised at all times for safety.
- Start with the beginner courses to build confidence before attempting more challenging routes.

2. Paragliding:

Experience the Black Forest from a unique perspective with a paragliding adventure. Tandem flights offer a safe and exhilarating way to soar above the stunning landscapes.

- Service Providers: Paragliding Schwarzwald.
- Average Cost: Tandem flights cost around $150 per person.

Tips:

- Book your flight in advance and choose a day with clear weather for the best experience.
- Wear comfortable, weather-appropriate clothing and sturdy shoes.

3. Zip Lining:

Zip lining through the Black Forest offers a thrilling way to experience the region's natural beauty. Several adventure parks in the area provide zip-lining courses that vary in length and difficulty.

- Service Providers: Available at Action Forest Kletterwald and other adventure parks.
- Average Cost: Included in the entry fee for adventure parks, ranging from $15 to $30.

Tips:

- Follow all safety instructions provided by the guides and ensure your harness is secure before starting.
- Enjoy the ride and take in the breathtaking views from high above the forest.

3.4.3 Family-Friendly Spots

Titisee-Neustadt is a fantastic destination for families, offering a variety of activities that cater to all ages. From fun-filled parks to educational museums, there's something for everyone to enjoy.

1. Badeparadies Schwarzwald:

Overview:

This large water park features numerous pools, water slides, and wellness areas.

- Address: Am Badeparadies 1, 79822 Titisee-Neustadt.
- Opening Times: Daily from 9 AM to 10 PM.
- Average Cost: Entry fees range from $20 to $30 for adults, and $15 to $25 for children, depending on the package.
- Tip: Arrive early to secure a good spot and avoid the afternoon rush. Bring your own towels to save on rental fees.

2. Mini Golf:

Titisee Mini Golf Park:

A fun activity for the whole family, featuring a well-maintained mini-golf course with beautiful views of the lake.

- Address: Seestraße 27, 79822 Titisee-Neustadt

- Opening Times: Daily from 10 AM to 6 PM (April to October).
- Average Cost: Around $5 per person.
- Tip: Play a round in the late afternoon when the temperatures are cooler and the course is less crowded.

3. Adventure Park:

Action Forest Kletterwald:

This adventure park offers various climbing and zip-lining courses for different age groups and skill levels.

- Address: Strandbadstraße 3, 79822 Titisee-Neustadt, +49 7652 1206.
- Opening Times: Daily from 9 AM to 6 PM (April to October).
- Average Cost: Entry fees range from $15 to $30, depending on the course.
- Tip: Wear comfortable athletic clothing and closed-toe shoes. Ensure children are supervised at all times for safety.

4. Educational Museums:

Spielzeugmuseum:

A toy museum showcasing a collection of antique toys and dolls, providing a nostalgic experience for adults and a fascinating one for kids.

- Address: Postplatz 5, 79822 Titisee-Neustadt.
- Opening Times: Tuesday to Sunday from 10 AM to 5 PM.
- Average Cost: Entry fees are around $7 for adults and $4 for children.

- Tip: Plan your visit on a weekday morning to avoid crowds and allow children to explore at their own pace.

5. Picnic Spots:

Hochfirstschanze:

This historic ski jump area provides a scenic spot for a family picnic, with plenty of space for children to play.

- Address: Hochfirstweg, 79822 Titisee-Neustadt.
- Tip: Bring a blanket, packed lunch, and some outdoor games. Dispose of trash responsibly to keep the area clean and enjoyable for everyone.

Titisee-Neustadt truly offers a comprehensive and enriching experience for travelers. Whether you're soaking in the serene beauty of Lake Titisee, embarking on thrilling outdoor adventures, or enjoying family-friendly activities, this destination promises unforgettable memories.

3.5 Off the Beaten Path

3.5.1 Hidden Gems

The Black Forest is more than just its famous towns and well-trodden trails. For the discerning traveler seeking an authentic experience, there are numerous hidden gems that offer a slice of local life, untouched by the usual tourist crowds. These spots provide an opportunity to delve deeper into the region's rich history, natural beauty, and cultural heritage.

1. Hiking to Geroldseck Castle Ruins

Nestled in the northern Black Forest near the town of Seelbach, the Geroldseck Castle Ruins are a perfect spot for history enthusiasts and hikers alike. Built in the 13th century, the castle once served as a significant stronghold but was destroyed in the 17th century during the Thirty Years' War. Today, the ruins stand as a picturesque reminder of the region's medieval past, surrounded by dense forests and offering spectacular views of the surrounding landscape.

Getting There and What to Expect

The hike to the ruins starts from the town of Seelbach. The trail is well-marked and takes about 1.5 hours one way. It's a moderate hike, suitable for most fitness levels. The path winds through serene forests, with the occasional clearing providing glimpses of the stunning countryside.

Cost and Tips

Hiking to Geroldseck Castle is free of charge. Remember to wear sturdy hiking boots and bring plenty of water, especially during the warmer months. The best time to visit is spring or autumn when the weather is mild, and the foliage is at its most beautiful.

2. Menzenschwander Waterfalls

Located near the village of Menzenschwand, these waterfalls are one of the Black Forest's best-kept secrets. Unlike the more famous Triberg Waterfalls, Menzenschwander is less crowded but equally, if not more, enchanting. The waterfalls are surrounded by lush greenery and offer a peaceful retreat from the hustle and bustle of more popular destinations.

How to Get There

Menzenschwand is a small village located about 15 kilometers from Titisee-Neustadt. The waterfalls are a short hike from the village center, making them easily accessible. There is ample parking available in the village.

Experience and Cost

The waterfalls are free to visit. The short hike to the falls takes about 20 minutes and is suitable for all ages. The trail is well-maintained and provides several viewpoints where you can stop and enjoy the scenery. It's a great spot for a picnic, so pack some snacks and enjoy the tranquility.

3. Ravennaschlucht (Ravenna Gorge)

For those who love a blend of natural beauty and historical intrigue, Ravennaschlucht offers a thrilling experience. This deep gorge is located near the town of Hinterzarten and is known for its dramatic scenery, with steep cliffs, rushing streams, and the impressive Ravenna Bridge, a railway viaduct that soars above the gorge.

Exploring the Gorge

The gorge can be explored via a network of hiking trails that range from easy walks to more challenging hikes. One of the most popular routes is the hike from Hinterzarten to the Hofgut Sternen, a historic inn located at the end of the gorge. This trail is about 6 kilometers long and takes around 2-3 hours to complete.

What to Bring and Costs

There's no entrance fee to explore the Ravennaschlucht. Comfortable hiking shoes and weather-appropriate clothing are recommended. During winter, parts of the gorge can be icy, so it's best visited in the warmer months.

3.5.2 Local Secrets

The true essence of the Black Forest lies in its lesser-known traditions, local flavors, and the warm hospitality of its residents. Discovering these local secrets can transform a good trip into an unforgettable one.

1. Wine Tasting in the Ortenau Region

While many travelers head straight for the bigger names in German wine, the Ortenau region offers a more intimate and equally delightful wine-tasting experience. Known for its excellent Rieslings and Spätburgunders, this area is dotted with family-run wineries that warmly welcome visitors.

Where to Go

One standout is the Alde Gott Winzer eG in Sasbachwalden. This cooperative winery produces a range of award-winning wines and offers guided tours and tastings. Visitors can explore the vineyards, learn about the winemaking process, and sample a selection of wines.

Cost and Experience

Tasting sessions typically cost around $15 per person, which includes a guided tour and several samples. Booking in advance is recommended, especially during the harvest season. The address is Alde Gott Winzer eG, Talstraße 2, 77887 Sasbachwalden. You can contact them at +49 7841 2071 or visit their website at www.aldegott.de.

2. Farm-to-Table Dining at Vogtsbauernhof

Experience traditional Black Forest cuisine with a modern twist at the Vogtsbauernhof open-air museum in Gutach. This museum not only showcases historic farmhouses but also features a delightful restaurant that serves dishes made with locally sourced ingredients.

Dining Details

The restaurant, located within the museum grounds, offers an array of regional specialties such as Black Forest ham, hearty soups, and delicious cakes. Dining here gives you a taste of the local food culture, all while enjoying the rustic ambiance of the museum.

Cost and Reservations

A meal at the museum's restaurant typically costs around $20-30 per person. The museum is located at Vogtsbauernhof, Vogtsbauernhof 1, 77793 Gutach. Opening hours are daily from 9:00 AM to 6:00 PM, with the restaurant operating within these hours. Reservations are recommended, especially on weekends and holidays. Visit www.vogtsbauernhof.de for more information.

3. Black Forest Cake Workshop in Todtmoos

No visit to the Black Forest is complete without indulging in its famous Black Forest cake. Take this experience a step further by learning how to make this iconic dessert yourself. In the town of Todtmoos, Café Zimmermann offers hands-on workshops where you can learn the secrets of baking an authentic Black Forest cake.

Workshop Experience

The workshop lasts about 3 hours and includes a detailed demonstration by the pastry chef, followed by a hands-on session where you get to create your own cake. At the end of the workshop, you can enjoy your creation with a cup of coffee or tea.

Cost and Booking

The cost for the workshop is approximately $50 per person, which includes all materials and ingredients. Workshops are held regularly, but it's advisable to book in advance. Contact Café Zimmermann at Hauptstraße 29, 79682 Todtmoos, or call +49 7674 634 to reserve your spot. More details can be found at www.cafe-zimmermann.de.

4. Local Beer Tasting in Alpirsbach

The Black Forest is not just about wine; it's also home to some excellent breweries. Alpirsbach, a small town known for its medieval monastery, is also famous for its brewery, Alpirsbacher Klosterbräu. A visit to this brewery offers a fascinating glimpse into the art of beer-making, along with generous tastings.

Brewery Tour

The brewery tour includes a visit to the brewing facilities, where you'll learn about the history of the brewery and the brewing process. The highlight, of course, is the tasting session, where you can sample a variety of their beers, from light lagers to rich, dark ales.

Cost and Practicalities

Tours cost around $10 per person and include multiple tastings. The brewery is located at Marktplatz 1, 72275 Alpirsbach. Tours are available Monday to Saturday, from 10:00 AM to 5:00 PM. Booking in advance is recommended, especially during peak tourist season. Visit www.alpirsbacher.de for more information.

5. Exploring the Caves of the Black Forest

For an adventurous and unique experience, explore the subterranean world of the Black Forest by visiting one of its many caves. The Erdmannshöhle in Hasel is one of the oldest accessible caves in Germany, known for its impressive stalactites and stalagmites.

Visiting Details

The cave is located near the town of Hasel and is easily accessible by car. Guided tours are available and provide fascinating insights into the cave's geology and history.

Cost and Timings

Admission to the cave is around $8 for adults and $5 for children. The cave is open from April to October, with tours running from 10:00 AM to 4:00 PM. Address: Erdmannshöhle, Erdmannshöhle 1, 79686 Hasel.

CHAPTER FOUR
NATURE AND OUTDOOR ACTIVITIES
4.1 Hiking Trails
4.1.1 Best Routes

The Black Forest offers a plethora of hiking trails that cater to all levels of hikers, from leisurely strolls to challenging mountain treks. Here are some of the best routes:

1. The Westweg Trail

- Length: 177 miles (285 km)
- Duration: Approximately 12-14 days
- Starting Point: Pforzheim
- Ending Point: Basel

The Westweg Trail is one of the oldest and most famous hiking trails in Germany. It runs from Pforzheim in the north to Basel in the south, traversing the entire Black Forest. The trail offers stunning views of dense forests, deep valleys, and picturesque villages. Along the way, hikers can enjoy the natural beauty of the region, including highlights like the Feldberg, the highest peak in the Black Forest, and the Titisee, a beautiful glacial lake.

Tips for Hiking the Westweg Trail:

- Accommodation: There are numerous guesthouses, inns, and hotels along the route. Booking in advance, especially during peak season, is advisable.
- Cost: Expect to spend around $50-$100 per night for accommodation. Meals in local restaurants will cost around $10-$30.

- Best Time to Hike: Late spring to early autumn (May to October) offers the best weather conditions.

2. The Albsteig Trail

- Length: 52 miles (83 km)
- Duration: Approximately 4-6 days
- Starting Point: Albbruck
- Ending Point: Feldberg

The Albsteig Trail, also known as the Alb Trail, is a shorter but equally rewarding hiking experience. This trail takes you through the heart of the Black Forest, offering panoramic views of the Upper Rhine Valley and the Alps. The route is known for its diverse landscapes, including rolling hills, dense forests, and serene meadows.

Tips for Hiking the Albsteig Trail:

- Accommodation: Small guesthouses and family-run hotels are available along the trail. Prices range from $40-$80 per night.
- Cost: Meals will cost approximately $10-$25. The trail is well-marked, so there's no need for a guide, which helps keep costs down.
- Best Time to Hike: Late spring to early autumn (May to October).

4.1.2 Difficulty Levels

Hiking in the Black Forest caters to all levels of fitness and experience. Trails are categorized into three main difficulty levels: easy, moderate, and difficult.

1. Easy Trails:

- Example: Ravenna Gorge Trail
- Length: 2.5 miles (4 km)

- Duration: 1-2 hours

Highlights: This trail is perfect for families and beginners. It features a picturesque gorge, a charming old stone bridge, and several small waterfalls. The trail is well-marked and relatively flat.

- Cost: Free

2. Moderate Trails:

- Example: Feldbergsteig Trail
- Length: 8 miles (13 km)
- Duration: 4-6 hours

Highlights: This trail takes you to the summit of the Feldberg, the highest peak in the Black Forest. The route offers stunning views of the surrounding mountains and valleys. Be prepared for some steep sections.

- Cost: Free

3. Difficult Trails:

- Example: Schluchtensteig Trail
- Length: 74 miles (119 km)
- Duration: 5-6 days

Highlights: This challenging trail takes you through some of the most rugged and remote parts of the Black Forest. It includes steep ascents, narrow paths, and spectacular gorges. This trail is recommended for experienced hikers.

- Cost: Accommodation costs range from $40-$100 per night.

4.2 Cycling Routes
4.2.1 Scenic Paths

Cycling is another fantastic way to explore the Black Forest. The region boasts numerous cycling paths that offer breathtaking scenery and a range of difficulty levels.

1. The Kinzig Valley Cycle Path

- Length: 57 miles (92 km)
- Duration: 2-3 days
- Starting Point: Freudenstadt
- Ending Point: Offenburg

The Kinzig Valley Cycle Path follows the course of the Kinzig River, passing through charming villages, vineyards, and picturesque landscapes. This route is relatively flat, making it suitable for families and casual cyclists.

Tips for Cycling the Kinzig Valley Path:

- Accommodation: Numerous bed and breakfasts and small hotels are available along the route. Prices range from $50-$90 per night.
- Cost: Bike rentals cost around $20-$30 per day. Meals will cost approximately $10-$25.
- Best Time to Cycle: Spring and autumn offer the best weather conditions.

2. The Schwarzwald Panorama Route

- Length: 43 miles (70 km)
- Duration: 2-3 days
- Starting Point: Pforzheim
- Ending Point: Waldshut

This route offers some of the most stunning panoramas in the Black Forest. It includes challenging climbs and exhilarating descents, making it ideal for experienced cyclists looking for a bit of adventure.

Tips for Cycling the Schwarzwald Panorama Route:

- Accommodation: Guesthouses and hotels are available along the route, with prices ranging from $50-$100 per night.
- Cost: Bike rentals cost around $20-$30 per day. Meals will cost approximately $10-$30.
- Best Time to Cycle: Spring and autumn offer the best weather conditions.

4.2.2 Bike Rentals

Renting a bike in the Black Forest is easy and affordable. Many towns and cities have rental shops that offer a variety of bikes, including mountain bikes, road bikes, and e-bikes.

Popular Bike Rental Shops:

1. Freiburg: Radstation Freiburg, Bismarckallee 1, 79098 Freiburg. Website: radstation-freiburg.de

- Cost: $20-$30 per day
- Amenities: Helmets, locks, and maps are usually included in the rental price.

2. Baden-Baden: Black Forest Bike, Lichtentaler Str. 1, 76530 Baden-Baden.

- Cost: $20-$30 per day
- Amenities: Helmets, locks, and maps are usually included in the rental price.

4.3 Winter Sports
4.3.1 Ski Resorts
The Black Forest is a popular destination for winter sports enthusiasts. The region offers several ski resorts that cater to all levels of skiers and snowboarders.

1. Feldberg Ski Resort

- Location: Feldberg, 79868 Feldberg
- Website: feldberg.de
- Opening Hours: 9:00 AM - 4:30 PM (December to April)
- Cost: Lift passes cost around $40-$60 per day.

Feldberg Ski Resort is the largest and most popular ski resort in the Black Forest. It offers a wide range of slopes for all skill levels, from beginner to advanced. The resort also has excellent facilities, including ski schools, equipment rentals, and several restaurants and cafes.

Tips for Skiing at Feldberg:

- Accommodation: There are numerous hotels and guesthouses in the Feldberg area. Prices range from $60-$150 per night.
- Amenities: On-site ski rentals, ski schools, and childcare facilities are available.
- Best Time to Visit: January to March offers the best snow conditions.

2. Todtnauberg Ski Resort

- Location: Todtnauberg, 79674 Todtnau
- Website: todtnauberg.info
- Opening Hours: 9:00 AM - 4:30 PM (December to April)

- Cost: Lift passes cost around $30-$50 per day.

Todtnauberg is a smaller, family-friendly ski resort with a more relaxed atmosphere. It offers a variety of slopes suitable for beginners and intermediate skiers. The resort also has a dedicated area for children and beginners, making it an excellent choice for families.

Tips for Skiing at Todtnauberg:

- Accommodation: Local guesthouses and small hotels are available. Prices range from $50-$120 per night.
- Amenities: On-site ski rentals, ski schools, and children's facilities are available.
- Best Time to Visit: January to March offers the best snow conditions.

4.3.2 *Snowboarding and Sledding*

Snowboarding and sledding are popular winter activities in the Black Forest. Many ski resorts offer dedicated areas and facilities for these activities.

1. Snowboarding at Belchen Ski Resort

- Location: Belchen, 79677 Aitern
- Website: belchen-seilbahn.de
- Opening Hours: 9:00 AM - 4:30 PM (December to April)
- Cost: Lift passes cost around $35-$55 per day.

Belchen Ski Resort offers excellent facilities for snowboarders, including well-groomed slopes and a terrain park with jumps and rails. The resort is known for its scenic beauty and offers a more relaxed atmosphere compared to larger resorts.

Tips for Snowboarding at Belchen:

- Accommodation: Guesthouses and hotels in the Belchen area range from $50-$130 per night.
- Amenities: On-site snowboard rentals and terrain park.
- Best Time to Visit: January to March for optimal snow conditions.

2. Sledding at Mehliskopf

- Location: Sandstraße 42, 76596 Forbach
- Website: mehliskopf.de
- Opening Hours: 9:00 AM - 4:30 PM (December to March)
- Cost: Sled rentals cost around $10-$15 per day.

Mehliskopf offers a fantastic sledding experience with dedicated sledding hills that are fun for all ages. The resort provides sled rentals and has a cozy lodge where you can warm up with hot drinks and snacks.

Tips for Sledding at Mehliskopf:

- Accommodation: Nearby guesthouses and inns offer lodging options ranging from $40-$100 per night.
- Amenities: Sled rentals and a lodge with food and drinks.
- Best Time to Visit: December to March for the best sledding conditions.

4.4 Adventure Activities
4.4.1 Zip Lining
Zip lining in the Black Forest offers a thrilling way to experience the region's stunning landscapes from a unique perspective.

1. Hirschgrund Zipline Area

- Location: 77728 Oppenau
- Website: hirschgrund-zipline.de
- Opening Hours: 10:00 AM - 6:00 PM (April to October)
- Cost: $50 per person

Hirschgrund Zipline Area is one of the largest zip line parks in Germany, featuring a series of seven zip lines that stretch over 2 miles. The longest zip line, at over 1,000 feet, offers breathtaking views of the surrounding forests and valleys.

Tips for Zip Lining at Hirschgrund:

- Booking: Advance booking is recommended, especially during weekends and holidays.
- Safety: All necessary safety equipment and instructions are provided.
- Best Time to Visit: Spring to autumn (April to October) for the best weather conditions.

2. Schwarzwald Hochseilgarten

- Location: Hinterlangenbach 31, 72270 Baiersbronn
- Opening Hours: 10:00 AM - 6:00 PM (April to October)
- Cost: $40 per person

Schwarzwald Hochseilgarten offers a combination of zip lines and high ropes courses, providing an exciting adventure for visitors of all ages. The park features multiple courses with varying difficulty levels, making it suitable for both beginners and experienced adventurers.

Tips for Zip Lining at Schwarzwald Hochseilgarten:

- Booking: Advance booking is recommended, especially during weekends and holidays.
- Safety: All necessary safety equipment and instructions are provided.
- Best Time to Visit: Spring to autumn (April to October) for the best weather conditions.

4.4.2 Paragliding

Paragliding in the Black Forest offers an exhilarating way to see the region's stunning landscapes from the sky.

1. Paragliding at Schauinsland

- Location: Schauinsland, 79100 Freiburg
- Website: flugschule-freiburg.de
- Opening Hours: 9:00 AM - 5:00 PM (April to October)
- Cost: $150 per person

Schauinsland is one of the best spots for paragliding in the Black Forest. The mountain offers ideal conditions for both beginners and experienced paragliders. Tandem flights are available for those new to the sport, providing a safe and memorable experience.

Tips for Paragliding at Schauinsland:

- Booking: Advance booking is required.
- Safety: All necessary safety equipment and instructions are provided. Tandem flights include an experienced pilot.
- Best Time to Visit: Spring to autumn (April to October) for the best weather conditions.

2. Paragliding at Kandel

- Location: Kandel, 79271 Sankt Peter
- Opening Hours: 9:00 AM - 5:00 PM (April to October)
- Cost: $150 per person

Kandel is another popular paragliding destination, offering breathtaking views of the Black Forest and the Rhine Valley. Tandem flights and paragliding courses are available for all skill levels.

Tips for Paragliding at Kandel:

- Booking: Advance booking is required.
- Safety: All necessary safety equipment and instructions are provided. Tandem flights include an experienced pilot.
- Best Time to Visit: Spring to autumn (April to October) for the best weather conditions.

4.5 Wildlife and Nature Parks

The Black Forest is home to a rich diversity of wildlife and numerous nature parks that offer excellent opportunities for wildlife watching and nature exploration.

1. Black Forest National Park

- Location: Schwarzwaldhochstraße 2, 77889 Seebach
- Website: nationalpark-schwarzwald.de
- Opening Hours: Open year-round
- Cost: Free

Black Forest National Park covers over 100 square miles and is home to a diverse range of flora and fauna. Visitors can explore numerous trails that wind through dense forests, past waterfalls, and across scenic ridges. The park offers guided tours, educational programs, and visitor centers with exhibits about the local ecology.

Tips for Visiting Black Forest National Park:

- Accommodation: There are several nearby towns with accommodation options ranging from $50-$150 per night.
- Activities: Hiking, wildlife watching, and educational tours are popular activities.
- Best Time to Visit: Spring to autumn for hiking and wildlife watching. Winter offers opportunities for snowshoeing and winter hikes.

2. Mundenhof Animal Park

- Location: Mundenhof 37, 79111 Freiburg
- Opening Hours: 9:00 AM - 6:00 PM (March to October), 9:00 AM - 4:00 PM (November to February)
- Cost: Free (donations welcome)

Mundenhof is a large animal park that focuses on the conservation of native and endangered species. The park features spacious enclosures and offers visitors the chance to see a variety of animals, including deer, wild boar, and birds of prey. There are also educational displays and interactive exhibits.

Tips for Visiting Mundenhof:

- Amenities: The park has picnic areas, a playground, and a small café.
- Activities: Animal watching, educational programs, and guided tours are available.

- Best Time to Visit: Spring to autumn offers the best weather for outdoor activities.

3. Wutach Gorge Nature Reserve

- Location: 79879 Wutach
- Website: wutachschlucht.de
- Opening Hours: Open year-round
- Cost: Free

Wutach Gorge is a stunning nature reserve known for its dramatic landscapes and rich biodiversity. The gorge features deep ravines, rushing rivers, and lush forests. It's a haven for hikers and nature enthusiasts, offering well-marked trails and spectacular scenery.

Tips for Visiting Wutach Gorge:

- Accommodation: Nearby towns offer a range of lodging options from $40-$100 per night.
- Activities: Hiking, bird watching, and nature photography are popular activities.
- Best Time to Visit: Spring to autumn for the best weather and trail conditions.

These activities provide a range of experiences that showcase the natural beauty and diverse landscapes of the Black Forest.

CHAPTER FIVE
CULTURAL EXPERIENCES

5.1 Black Forest Villages

The Black Forest, or Schwarzwald, is a treasure trove of picturesque villages and towns, each offering a unique window into the region's rich cultural heritage, traditions, and architectural marvels. Exploring these villages is like stepping back in time, where history comes alive through vibrant festivals, ancient buildings, and local customs. Here's an in-depth look at some of the most enchanting Black Forest villages and what makes them special.

5.1.1 Traditions and Festivals

1. Fasnet: The Swabian-Alemannic Carnival

One of the most anticipated events in the Black Forest calendar is Fasnet, the Swabian-Alemannic carnival. This traditional pre-Lenten festival, which dates back centuries, is celebrated with great enthusiasm in towns and villages across the region. Fasnet is characterized by colorful parades, elaborate costumes, and a joyous, sometimes mischievous, atmosphere.

2. Rottweil Narrensprung

Rottweil, the oldest town in Baden-Württemberg, is renowned for its Narrensprung, or Fool's Leap, a highlight of the Fasnet celebrations. During this event, which takes place on Fasnet Monday, participants known as Narren don traditional wooden masks and costumes representing various characters from folklore, including witches, jesters, and forest spirits. The parade begins early in the morning and winds through the narrow streets of the town, accompanied by the sound of drums and trumpets.

To fully enjoy the Narrensprung, it's recommended to arrive early, as the streets fill up quickly with locals and tourists eager to witness the spectacle. The event is free to attend, but securing a good viewing spot is essential for capturing the best photos and enjoying the performances.

3. Villingen-Schwenningen Fasnet

Villingen-Schwenningen, another town with deep-rooted Fasnet traditions, hosts a series of parades and events leading up to Ash Wednesday. The town's Fasnet guilds, or Narrenzünfte, play a central role in organizing the festivities. Each guild has its own unique costumes and rituals, contributing to the vibrant and diverse atmosphere of the celebrations.

One of the key events is the Katzenmusik, or Cat Music parade, which takes place on the evening of Fasnet Monday. Participants dressed in whimsical and often grotesque costumes march through the streets, creating a cacophony of sounds with drums, horns, and other instruments. This tradition is believed to chase away evil spirits and welcome the arrival of spring.

Black Forest Christmas Markets

The Black Forest region transforms into a winter wonderland during the holiday season, with Christmas markets that capture the magic and spirit of the season. These markets, or Weihnachtsmärkte, are held in towns and villages throughout the region, offering a delightful experience for visitors of all ages.

1. Freiburg Christmas Market

Located at the heart of Freiburg's historic Old Town, the Freiburg Christmas Market is one of the largest and most popular in the Black Forest. Open daily from late November to December 23, the market features over 100 stalls selling handmade crafts, festive decorations, and seasonal treats. Visitors can indulge in traditional foods like bratwurst, roasted chestnuts, and lebkuchen (gingerbread cookies), while sipping on glühwein (mulled wine) to keep warm.

A highlight of the Freiburg Christmas Market is the large, beautifully decorated Christmas tree in Rathausplatz, which serves as the centerpiece of the festivities. The market is open from 10 AM to 8:30 PM, with extended hours on weekends. Admission is free, but budgeting around $20-30 for food and small purchases is advisable.

2. Gengenbach Christmas Market

The Gengenbach Christmas Market is famous for its giant Advent calendar, where each window of the town hall is transformed into an artistic depiction of a holiday scene. Every evening at 6 PM, a new window is revealed with great fanfare, accompanied by music and storytelling.

In addition to the Advent calendar, the market offers a charming array of stalls selling local crafts, Christmas ornaments, and delicious treats. The market is open from late November to December 23, from 11 AM to 8 PM on weekdays and 11 AM to 9 PM on weekends. The festive atmosphere and unique attractions make the Gengenbach Christmas Market a must-visit during the holiday season.

Traditional Harvest Festivals

Harvest festivals, known as Erntedankfest, are an important part of Black Forest culture, celebrating the bounty of the land and the end of the agricultural season. These festivals typically take place in late September or early October and feature a blend of religious ceremonies, parades, and communal feasts.

1. Bühl Harvest Festival

The town of Bühl, located at the foot of the Black Forest, hosts one of the region's most vibrant harvest festivals. The Bühl Harvest Festival includes a grand parade with floats decorated with fruits, vegetables, and flowers, symbolizing the abundance of the harvest. Local farmers, craftsmen, and community groups participate in the parade, dressed in traditional attire.

The festival also features a bustling market where visitors can purchase fresh produce, artisanal products, and homemade delicacies. Live music, folk dances, and cultural performances add to the festive atmosphere. The Bühl Harvest Festival is typically held over a weekend, with events running from Friday evening to Sunday afternoon. Admission is free, but bring cash for purchases at the market stalls.

2. Cuckoo Clock Festival in Schonach

The Black Forest is famous for its cuckoo clocks, and the town of Schonach is at the heart of this tradition. Every two years, Schonach hosts the Cuckoo Clock Festival, a celebration of the craftsmanship and heritage of these iconic timepieces. The festival attracts clock enthusiasts from around the world and features a variety of activities, including clock-making demonstrations, guided tours of local workshops, and a cuckoo clock parade.

During the festival, visitors can learn about the history and intricate process of cuckoo clock production, from the carving of wooden components to the assembly of the mechanical movements. The festival also includes a competition for the most creative and beautifully crafted cuckoo clocks, with prizes awarded by a panel of experts.

The Cuckoo Clock Festival typically takes place over a weekend in late June. Admission to the festival is free, but some workshops and guided tours may charge a small fee. The festival provides a unique opportunity to immerse yourself in one of the Black Forest's most enduring traditions.

Traditional Village Festivals

Throughout the year, villages in the Black Forest host a variety of smaller festivals that celebrate local customs, music, and culinary traditions. These village festivals offer an intimate and authentic experience, allowing visitors to connect with the local community and participate in age-old traditions.

1. Simonswald Flammkuchen Festival

Simonswald, a picturesque village nestled in the Elz Valley, is known for its annual Flammkuchen Festival. Flammkuchen, also known as tarte flambée, is a traditional Alsatian dish consisting of a thin, crispy dough topped with crème fraîche, onions, and bacon. The festival celebrates this regional specialty with a variety of Flammkuchen recipes, from classic to innovative toppings.

Visitors can watch as local bakers prepare Flammkuchen in wood-fired ovens, and sample different variations of the dish. The festival also features live music, folk dances, and a market selling local crafts and products. The Simonswald Flammkuchen Festival is typically held in early September, and admission is free. Expect to spend around $10-15 for a hearty portion of Flammkuchen and a drink.

2. Schiltach Medieval Festival

Schiltach, a town known for its well-preserved medieval architecture, hosts a Medieval Festival that transports visitors back in time. The festival features reenactments of historical events, jousting tournaments, and performances by minstrels and acrobats. Visitors can explore a medieval market with stalls selling handmade goods, traditional foods, and beverages.

Participants, both locals and performers, dress in period costumes, adding to the authenticity of the event. The festival also includes workshops where visitors can try their hand at traditional crafts like blacksmithing, pottery, and archery.

The Schiltach Medieval Festival is usually held in mid-August, over a weekend. Admission costs around $10 for adults and $5 for children, with additional fees for certain activities and workshops. The festival provides a fascinating glimpse into the region's medieval history and offers fun for the whole family.

5.1.2 Architecture and Heritage
1. Half-Timbered Houses (Fachwerkhäuser)

The half-timbered houses are the most iconic architectural feature of the Black Forest. These structures, known as Fachwerkhäuser, are distinguished by their timber frames with interspersed white plaster or brick, often arranged in intricate patterns. These houses date back to the medieval period and are still maintained with great care, preserving their historical charm.

Schiltach is one of the best-preserved towns for viewing these houses. Nestled along the Kinzig River, Schiltach's marketplace is surrounded by beautifully restored half-timbered houses. Walking through the narrow, cobbled streets, one can't help but feel transported back in time. Key buildings to visit include the Marktplatz and the Apothekenmuseum, a pharmacy museum showcasing centuries-old pharmaceutical practices.

Haslach im Kinzigtal is another gem with an old town filled with these picturesque houses. The town's history as a significant trading post is reflected in its architecture. Notable sights include the Hansjakob Museum located in a former town mill, showcasing local history and literature. The museum is open from Tuesday to Sunday, 10 AM to 4 PM, and admission is $5 for adults.

To fully appreciate the craftsmanship, consider staying in a historic guesthouse. Many of these buildings have been converted into charming accommodations, like the Hotel Gasthaus Sonne in Schiltach, offering a blend of historical ambiance and modern comforts.

2. Historic Farmhouses

The Black Forest is also renowned for its historic farmhouses, known as Schwarzwaldhäuser. These large, wooden structures were built to withstand the harsh weather conditions of the region, featuring steeply pitched roofs to shed snow and wide eaves to protect the walls from rain.

Vogtsbauernhof, located in Gutach, is part of the Black Forest Open Air Museum. This museum offers an immersive experience into rural life in the Black Forest over the centuries. The farmhouses here are meticulously preserved and furnished, showcasing traditional living conditions, agricultural practices, and craftsmanship. The museum also hosts workshops where visitors can learn about traditional crafts like blacksmithing and weaving. Open from March to November, 10 AM to 6 PM, admission is $10 for adults and $5 for children.

Hofgut Sternen in Breitnau is another significant site. This complex includes a traditional Black Forest farmhouse, a glassblowing workshop, and a hotel. It's a fantastic place to see traditional architecture and buy handmade souvenirs. The glassblowing demonstrations are particularly fascinating, allowing visitors to see skilled artisans at work. The complex is open year-round, and entry is free, though there are charges for specific activities like glassblowing workshops.

3. Baroque and Rococo Churches

The Black Forest is dotted with churches that reflect the Baroque and Rococo architectural styles, which flourished in the 17th and 18th centuries. These churches are not only places of worship but also masterpieces of art and architecture, adorned with elaborate decorations, frescoes, and altarpieces.

St. Peter's Abbey in St. Peter im Schwarzwald is a stunning example of Baroque architecture. The abbey church, built between 1724 and 1727, features a richly decorated interior with ornate stuccoes, frescoes by Franz Joseph Spiegler, and a high altar by Johann Christian Wentzinger. The abbey is still active and offers guided tours that provide insight into its history and art. The church is open daily from 8 AM to 6 PM, and admission is free.

Ettlingen Palace near Karlsruhe, although not a church, houses a beautiful chapel that exemplifies the Rococo style. The palace itself, originally a medieval castle, was transformed in the 18th century into a Baroque residence.

The chapel is adorned with frescoes, gilded stucco, and a magnificent altar. Visitors can tour the palace and chapel, with admission costing $10 for adults.

Kloster Maulbronn, a former Cistercian monastery and a UNESCO World Heritage site, combines Gothic and Romanesque elements with later Baroque additions. The monastery complex is remarkably well-preserved, offering a comprehensive view of monastic life over the centuries. The monastery is open year-round, with guided tours available for $12.

4. Castles and Palaces

The Black Forest is home to numerous castles and palaces that reflect the region's feudal past and architectural evolution. These structures, often perched on hills or surrounded by dense forests, offer panoramic views and a deep dive into the history of the region's nobility.

Hohenzollern Castle, located near the town of Hechingen, is one of the most impressive castles in Germany. This fortress has been the ancestral seat of the Prussian Kings and German Emperors. The castle's architecture is a mix of medieval and 19th-century styles, featuring grand halls, beautiful gardens, and a treasury with historical artifacts. Open daily from 10 AM to 5:30 PM, admission is $15 for adults and $10 for children. Guided tours, which cost an additional $5, provide detailed insights into the castle's history and architecture.

Rotteln Castle, near Lörrach, is a medieval fortress that offers spectacular views of the surrounding area. The ruins, which date back to the 11th century, include a well-preserved keep and defensive walls. The castle is open from April to October, daily from 9 AM to 6 PM. Admission is $5 for adults and $2.50 for children. The annual medieval festival, held in the summer, is a highlight, featuring reenactments, markets, and entertainment.

New Palace in Baden-Baden (Neues Schloss) is another architectural marvel. Originally built in the Renaissance style, it was later expanded and renovated in the Baroque style. The palace overlooks the town and offers stunning views of the Black Forest. While the palace itself is currently being restored and not open to the public, the gardens and grounds are accessible. The nearby Altes Schloss (Old Castle), also in Baden-Baden, is open to visitors and offers breathtaking views from its towers. Entry to the Old Castle is free, and it's open year-round from 8 AM to dusk.

5. Museums and Heritage Centers

To delve deeper into the architectural and cultural heritage of the Black Forest, visiting local museums and heritage centers is essential. These institutions offer exhibitions, artifacts, and educational programs that illuminate various aspects of the region's history.

The Black Forest Museum (Schwarzwaldmuseum) in Triberg provides an extensive overview of the region's cultural history. Exhibits include traditional costumes, musical instruments, and a large collection of Black Forest clocks. The museum also features reconstructed rooms from historical Black Forest houses, giving visitors a sense of life in the past. The museum is open daily from 10 AM to 5 PM, and admission is $7 for adults and $3.50 for children.

The German Clock Museum (Deutsches Uhrenmuseum) in Furtwangen is a must-visit for anyone interested in the Black Forest's famous clock-making tradition. The museum boasts over 8,000 timepieces, ranging from early sundials to modern wristwatches. Interactive exhibits and guided tours provide insights into the craftsmanship and technological advancements in horology. Open daily from 9 AM to 6 PM, admission is $8 for adults and $4 for children.

The Monastery and Palace Museum in St. Blasien (Kloster- und Schlossmuseum) offers a fascinating look at the architectural and religious history of this former Benedictine abbey. The museum's exhibits include religious artifacts, historical documents, and models of the monastery complex. The adjacent domed church, one of the largest in Europe, is an architectural highlight. The museum is open from April to October, Tuesday to Sunday, 10 AM to 5 PM, with an admission fee of $5.

6. Hidden Architectural Gems

While the well-known sites attract many visitors, the Black Forest is also home to lesser-known architectural treasures that are worth exploring.

The Hexenloch Mill (Hexenlochmühle) in Furtwangen is a charming historical mill located in a picturesque valley. This mill, still in operation, showcases traditional milling techniques and features a small museum. The adjacent restaurant offers hearty Black Forest cuisine, making it a perfect stop for lunch. The mill is open daily from 10 AM to 5 PM, and entry is free.

The Windeck Castle Ruins (Burgruine Windeck) near Bühl provide a fascinating glimpse into medieval architecture. The ruins, perched on a hilltop, include a well-preserved tower and defensive walls. The site is accessible via a short hike, and the views from the top are breathtaking. Open year-round, entry to the ruins is free.

The Staufen Castle Ruins (Burgruine Staufen) overlooking the town of Staufen im Breisgau are another hidden gem. The castle, associated with the legendary Faust, offers stunning views of the Rhine Valley and the Black Forest. The ruins are accessible by a short hike from the town center, and entry is free.

5.2 Museums and Galleries

The Black Forest is not only known for its stunning natural beauty but also for its rich cultural heritage. The region boasts a plethora of museums and galleries that cater to a variety of interests, from art and history to local traditions and innovations. Here, we delve into some of the must-visit exhibitions and highlight the contributions of local artists, ensuring you get a comprehensive cultural experience during your visit.

5.2.1 Must-Visit Exhibitions

1. Black Forest Open Air Museum Vogtsbauernhof

Located in Gutach, the Black Forest Open Air Museum Vogtsbauernhof offers a fascinating glimpse into rural life over the centuries. This living museum comprises several historic farmhouses, barns, and mills, all authentically furnished to reflect different periods and regions of the Black Forest.

- Address: Wählerbrücke 1, 77793 Gutach
- Opening Hours: March to November, daily from 10 AM to 6 PM
- Admission: $10 for adults, $5 for children

Each farmhouse tells a unique story about the people who lived there, their customs, and their daily activities. You can see traditional crafts in action, such as basket weaving, blacksmithing, and bread baking. The museum also hosts seasonal events and workshops, providing interactive experiences for visitors of all ages. To make the most of your visit, plan to spend at least half a day exploring the various buildings and attending demonstrations.

2. Frieder Burda Museum

Art enthusiasts will find the Frieder Burda Museum in Baden-Baden a treasure trove of modern and contemporary art. Founded by art collector Frieder Burda, the museum features works by renowned artists such as Pablo Picasso, Jackson Pollock, and Gerhard Richter.

- Address: Lichtentaler Allee 8b, 76530 Baden-Baden
- Opening Hours: Tuesday to Sunday, 10 AM to 6 PM
- Admission: $15 for adults, discounts for students and seniors

The museum's striking architecture, designed by Richard Meier, perfectly complements its impressive collection. In addition to its permanent exhibits, the Frieder Burda Museum hosts temporary exhibitions that bring in masterpieces from around the world. Audio guides are available in multiple languages, offering deeper insights into the artworks on display. Allocate a few hours to fully appreciate the diverse range of art and the serene setting of Lichtentaler Allee.

3. German Clock Museum

The German Clock Museum in Furtwangen is a must-visit for those intrigued by horology and the Black Forest's famous clock-making tradition. The museum boasts a collection of over 8,000 timepieces, including iconic cuckoo clocks, intricate pocket watches, and modern chronometers.

- Address: Robert-Gerwig-Platz 1, 78120 Furtwangen
- Opening Hours: Daily from 9 AM to 6 PM
- Admission: $8 for adults, $4 for children

Visitors can explore the evolution of timekeeping devices, from ancient sundials to contemporary atomic clocks. Interactive displays and detailed descriptions provide a comprehensive understanding of the technological advancements and artistic craftsmanship involved in clockmaking. Don't miss the demonstration of a large musical clock, which plays a charming melody at regular intervals. To enhance your experience, consider joining a guided tour, which is included in the admission fee.

4. Hohenbaden Castle (Old Castle)

For history buffs, Hohenbaden Castle, also known as the Old Castle, offers a fascinating journey into the medieval past. Perched on a hilltop overlooking Baden-Baden, the castle was built in the 12th century and provides panoramic views of the surrounding landscape.

- Address: Alter Schlossweg 10, 76532 Baden-Baden
- Opening Hours: Daily from 8 AM to 8 PM
- Admission: Free

Although partially in ruins, the castle retains much of its original charm. Visitors can explore the remains of the great hall, the watchtower, and the chapel. Information panels throughout the site offer historical context and insights into the castle's construction and significance. The highlight of the visit is the climb to the top of the keep, where you'll be rewarded with breathtaking views of the Black Forest and the Rhine Valley. It's a great spot for photography, so be sure to bring your camera.

5. Hans Thoma Art Museum

The Hans Thoma Art Museum in Bernau celebrates the life and works of Hans Thoma, a prominent painter born in the Black Forest. The museum features a diverse collection of Thoma's landscapes, portraits, and still lifes, alongside temporary exhibitions of contemporary artists.

- Address: Am Kurpark 1, 79872 Bernau im Schwarzwald
- Opening Hours: Wednesday to Sunday, 10 AM to 5 PM
- Admission: $7 for adults, $3.50 for children

Hans Thoma's art is known for its vivid depiction of nature and rural life, often inspired by the scenic beauty of the Black Forest. The museum also offers workshops and lectures, providing deeper insights into Thoma's techniques and the cultural context of his work. Spend a couple of hours here to fully appreciate the artist's contributions and the tranquil setting of Bernau.

6. Kunsthalle Messmer

Kunsthalle Messmer in Riegel is a contemporary art gallery housed in a beautifully restored industrial building. The gallery showcases works by both established and emerging artists, offering a diverse range of styles and mediums.

- Address: Hauptstraße 57, 79359 Riegel am Kaiserstuhl
- Opening Hours: Wednesday to Sunday, 11 AM to 5 PM
- Admission: $10 for adults, $5 for students

The gallery's exhibitions change regularly, ensuring there's always something new to see. Past exhibitions have featured abstract art, sculpture, and installations that challenge conventional perspectives. The gallery also hosts artist talks and guided tours, which provide valuable insights into the creative process. Plan to spend an afternoon here, exploring the thought-provoking artworks and enjoying the serene surroundings of Riegel.

5.2.2 Local Artists

1. Hans Thoma

Hans Thoma is one of the Black Forest's most celebrated artists, known for his landscapes that capture the region's natural beauty. Born in Bernau in 1839, Thoma's work is characterized by its detailed and vibrant depiction of rural scenes and local life. The Hans Thoma Art Museum in Bernau is dedicated to his legacy, showcasing a comprehensive collection of his paintings.

Visitors can see Thoma's evolution as an artist, from his early works influenced by Romanticism to his later pieces that reflect his mature style. The museum also offers insight into Thoma's personal life and his connection to the Black Forest. Special exhibitions and events are held throughout the year, focusing on various aspects of his work and his impact on the art world.

2. Local Studios and Workshops

The Black Forest is home to many talented artists and craftsmen who draw inspiration from the region's landscapes and traditions. Visiting local studios and workshops offers a unique opportunity to meet these artists and see their creative process firsthand. Many of these studios are located in picturesque villages, adding to the charm of the experience.

For example, the glassblowing studio Dorotheenhütte in Wolfach allows visitors to watch artisans create intricate glass pieces using traditional techniques. You can even try your hand at glassblowing and create your own souvenir. The studio is open daily from 9 AM to 5 PM, and prices for workshops start at $25.

In addition to glassblowing, the Black Forest is known for its woodcarving. The town of Triberg is famous for its cuckoo clocks, and many workshops offer demonstrations and tours. The House of 1000 Clocks is a popular destination, where you can see a wide variety of clocks and learn about the history of this unique craft. The shop is open daily from 10 AM to 6 PM, and prices for handmade clocks vary.

3. Art Fairs and Markets

Art fairs and markets are excellent places to discover local talent and purchase unique artworks. The Freiburg Art Fair, held annually in June, features a wide range of contemporary art, from paintings and sculptures to photography and mixed media. The fair attracts artists from all over the region and offers a vibrant atmosphere for art lovers to explore and purchase pieces.

Another notable event is the Baden-Baden International Art Fair, which takes place every September. This prestigious event showcases works by established and emerging artists, with a focus on modern and contemporary art. The fair includes exhibitions, live performances, and workshops, providing a comprehensive cultural experience.

5.3 Music and Performing Arts
5.3.1 Concerts and Events
The Black Forest hosts a vibrant array of music and performing arts events throughout the year. The Baden-Baden Festspielhaus, Europe's second-largest opera and concert hall, offers a rich program of opera, ballet, and classical music. The Festspielhaus is renowned for its acoustics and opulent architecture, making it a premier destination for music lovers. Ticket prices vary depending on the performance, ranging from $50 to $200. The venue is located at Beim Alten Bahnhof 2, Baden-Baden, and it's advisable to book tickets in advance through their website.

The Schwarzwald Musikfestival is another highlight, held annually across various locations in the Black Forest. This festival features a diverse lineup of classical concerts, jazz performances, and folk music, bringing together local and international artists. Performances are often held in unique venues, such as historic churches, open-air stages, and even in the heart of the forest. Ticket prices range from $20 to $60, and the festival runs from May to June.

For a more intimate setting, consider attending a performance at the Konzerthaus Freiburg. This venue hosts a variety of concerts, from chamber music to symphonies, often featuring the Freiburg Philharmonic Orchestra. The concert hall is located at Konrad-Adenauer-Platz 1, Freiburg, with ticket prices typically between $30 and $80.

5.3.2 Traditional Music
Traditional music is an integral part of Black Forest culture, often performed at local festivals, events, and in village squares. The sound of alphorns, accordions, and zither fills the air, creating a nostalgic atmosphere. One of the best

places to experience this is at the Echte Schwarzwälder Volksmusikabend, an evening of traditional Black Forest music held in various towns.

In addition to scheduled performances, many local taverns and inns feature live folk music, particularly on weekends. The Gasthof zum Lamm in St. Peter is a popular spot, where you can enjoy hearty local dishes while listening to musicians play traditional tunes. Prices for meals at these establishments typically range from $15 to $30.

For a deeper understanding of traditional music, visit the Black Forest Folk Music Archive in Freiburg. This archive preserves and promotes the region's musical heritage, offering workshops, lectures, and exhibitions. It's located at Rathausgasse 33, Freiburg, and is open Monday to Friday, 10 AM to 4 PM. Entry is free, but donations are welcome.

5.4 Local Cuisine and Dining

The culinary landscape of the Black Forest is as rich and varied as its scenery. From hearty regional dishes and world-renowned desserts to exceptional wines and craft beers, the gastronomy here is a true reflection of the region's culture and history. In this chapter, we'll take a closer look at the culinary delights of the Black Forest, providing a guide to the must-try dishes, the best restaurants, and the top spots for wine tasting and breweries.

5.4.1 Regional Dishes

The Black Forest is famed for its robust, flavorful dishes that make the most of local produce. Here are some of the key culinary highlights:

1. Schwarzwälder Schinken (Black Forest Ham): This smoked ham is perhaps the most famous product of the Black Forest. Cured with a blend of spices and then cold-

smoked over fir wood, it has a distinctive flavor that is both savory and slightly sweet. It's typically served thinly sliced with bread, pickles, and mustard. You can find authentic Black Forest ham at local markets and many restaurants. A platter of Black Forest ham at a local eatery such as Gasthaus Löwen in Titisee-Neustadt will cost around $10-15.

2. Maultaschen: Often referred to as Swabian ravioli, Maultaschen are pasta squares filled with a mixture of minced meat, spinach, onions, and spices. They can be served in broth, pan-fried with onions, or topped with melted cheese. This dish is believed to have been created by monks who wanted to hide meat during Lent, earning it the nickname "Herrgottsbescheißerle" (God cheaters). A hearty serving of Maultaschen at a traditional restaurant will set you back about $12-18.

3. Schwarzwälder Kirschtorte (Black Forest Cake): This iconic dessert is a masterpiece of layers—chocolate sponge cake soaked in Kirsch (cherry brandy), whipped cream, and cherries, all topped with chocolate shavings. Almost every café and bakery in the Black Forest has its version, but Café Schäfer in Triberg is particularly renowned for its Black Forest Cake, costing about $5-7 per slice.

4. Sauerbraten: This pot roast is marinated for several days in a mixture of vinegar, water, and spices before being slow-cooked to perfection. It's traditionally served with red cabbage and potato dumplings. The combination of sweet, sour, and savory flavors makes Sauerbraten a must-try. A plate of Sauerbraten at a traditional restaurant like Gasthaus Zum Wilden Esel in Freiburg will cost around $20-25.

5. Flammkuchen: Known as "tarte flambée" in French, this Alsatian dish is similar to pizza but with a thinner, crispier crust. It's typically topped with crème fraîche, onions, and

bacon. You can find variations with additional toppings like cheese, mushrooms, or herbs. Enjoying a Flammkuchen at a local tavern will cost approximately $10-15.

6. Spätzle: These soft egg noodles are a staple in Swabian cuisine and can be served as a side dish or as a main course. They are often topped with cheese and fried onions (Käsespätzle) or served with a rich gravy. A generous portion of Käsespätzle at a traditional inn will cost around $12-18.

5.4.2 Best Restaurants

The Black Forest region is home to a diverse range of dining experiences, from Michelin-starred restaurants to charming village inns. Here are ten recommended restaurants that offer an exceptional taste of the local cuisine:

1. Restaurant Bareiss, Baiersbronn

- Cuisine: Fine Dining, Regional
- Highlights: Three Michelin stars, exquisite tasting menus, focus on local ingredients
- Cost: Around $200 per person
- Address: Hermine-Bareiss-Weg 1, 72270 Baiersbronn-Mitteltal

Restaurant Bareiss is a culinary destination in itself, offering a refined dining experience with a focus on regional ingredients. The tasting menu showcases dishes like venison with elderflower and hazelnut, and trout with horseradish and beetroot. The elegant setting and impeccable service make it a must-visit.

2. Schwarzwaldstube at Hotel Traube Tonbach, Baiersbronn

- Cuisine: Fine Dining, Gourmet

- Highlights: Three Michelin stars, creative culinary techniques, seasonal menus
- Cost: Around $200-250 per person
- Address: Tonbachstraße 237, 72270 Baiersbronn

Schwarzwaldstube is renowned for its creative approach to Black Forest cuisine, using seasonal ingredients to craft dishes that are both innovative and deeply rooted in tradition. The setting is luxurious, and the service is top-notch.

3. Restaurant Adler, Häusern

- Cuisine: Fine Dining, Regional
- Highlights: One Michelin star, traditional Black Forest flavors, intimate setting
- Cost: Around $100-150 per person
- Address: In der Wässere 1, 79837 Häusern

This Michelin-starred restaurant offers a refined take on regional cuisine. The menu features dishes like roast venison with juniper and apple, and trout from local streams. The cozy, intimate atmosphere adds to the charm.

4. Zum Wilden Esel, Freiburg

- Cuisine: Traditional German
- Highlights: Hearty regional dishes, rustic ambiance, seasonal menu
- Cost: $20-40 per meal
- Address: Schützenallee 12, 79102 Freiburg

Zum Wilden Esel is a rustic tavern known for its hearty traditional fare. Specialties include Sauerbraten and Maultaschen, and the menu changes seasonally to reflect the freshest local ingredients. The cozy setting and friendly service make it a favorite among locals.

5. Gasthaus Löwen, Titisee-Neustadt

- Cuisine: Traditional German, Regional
- Highlights: Charming inn, Black Forest ham, Flammkuchen
- Cost: $15-30 per meal
- Address: Hauptstraße 23, 79822 Titisee-Neustadt

Located near Lake Titisee, this charming inn offers a delightful menu of regional dishes, including Black Forest ham and Flammkuchen. The cozy setting and friendly service make it a favorite among locals and tourists alike.

6. Restaurant zum Kreuz, St. Märgen

- Cuisine: Traditional German, Regional
- Highlights: Farm-to-table dining, seasonal dishes, scenic views
- Cost: $20-40 per meal
- Address: Hauptstraße 1, 79274 St. Märgen

This restaurant prides itself on farm-to-table dining, using ingredients sourced from local farms and forests. The seasonal menu features dishes like wild boar stew and trout from local streams. The restaurant also offers scenic views of the surrounding countryside.

7. Gasthof zum Rössle, Elzach

- Cuisine: Traditional German, Regional
- Highlights: Family-run inn, homemade sausages, traditional Black Forest dishes
- Cost: $15-30 per meal
- Address: Kirchstraße 1, 79215 Elzach

A family-run inn, Gasthof zum Rössle offers traditional Black Forest hospitality and cuisine. The menu features homemade sausages, Sauerbraten, and seasonal specialties. The warm, welcoming atmosphere makes it a great place to enjoy a traditional meal.

8. Schloss Eberstein, Gernsbach

- Cuisine: Fine Dining, Regional
- Highlights: Historic castle setting, gourmet cuisine, excellent wine selection
- Cost: $100-150 per person
- Address: Schloss Eberstein 1, 76593 Gernsbach

Set in a historic castle, Schloss Eberstein offers a dining experience that combines gourmet cuisine with a touch of history. The menu features regional and seasonal dishes, and the wine list is extensive, featuring many local wines.

9. Gasthaus zum Engel, Todtnau

- Cuisine: Traditional German, Regional
- Highlights: Cozy inn, traditional Black Forest dishes, homemade desserts
- Cost: $15-30 per meal
- Address: Hauptstraße 14, 79674 Todtnau

Gasthaus zum Engel is a cozy inn known for its traditional Black Forest dishes and homemade desserts. The menu includes classics like Maultaschen and Spätzle, and the inn's warm atmosphere makes it a perfect place for a relaxing meal.

10. Hotel Sackmann, Baiersbronn

- Cuisine: Fine Dining, Gourmet

- Highlights: Elegant setting, seasonal and regional cuisine, excellent service
- Cost: $100-200 per person
- Address: Murgtalstraße 602, 72270 Baiersbronn

Hotel Sackmann offers an elegant dining experience with a focus on seasonal and regional cuisine. The menu changes regularly to highlight the freshest ingredients, and the service is impeccable. The beautiful setting adds to the overall experience.

5.4.3 Wine Tasting and Breweries

The Black Forest region is also renowned for its exceptional wines and beers. Here are the top spots for wine tasting and breweries:

1. Franz Keller Winery, Oberbergen: Located in the Kaiserstuhl region, this family-run winery is famous for its Pinot Noirs and Chardonnays. The winery offers guided tours that include a walk through the vineyards and a tasting session. Tastings cost around $15-20, and the winery is open Monday to Saturday, 10 AM to 6 PM. Booking in advance is recommended and can be done via their website or by calling +49 7662 93130. Address: Franz Keller Schwarzer Adler, Badbergstraße 23, 79235 Vogtsburg.

2. Weingut Dr. Heger, Ihringen: Another standout in the Kaiserstuhl region, Weingut Dr. Heger specializes in premium wines that reflect the unique terroir of the area. The winery offers tastings by appointment, with prices starting at $15 per person. The tasting room is open Monday to Saturday, 10 AM to 5 PM. Reservations can be made by calling +49 7668 9020. Address: Hinter den Zäunen 1, 79241 Ihringen.

3. Rothaus Brewery, Grafenhausen: This historic brewery, founded in 1791, is famous for its Tannenzäpfle beer. The brewery offers guided tours that include a walk through the brewing process, followed by a tasting session. Tours cost $10 per person and are available Monday to Friday, 10 AM to 4 PM. Reservations can be made on their website or by calling +49 7748 5220. Address: Rothaus 1, 79865 Grafenhausen.

4. Badische Staatsbrauerei Rothaus, Rothaus: Located in the heart of the Black Forest, this state-owned brewery produces some of Germany's finest beers. The brewery tour includes a visit to the production facilities and a tasting session in their cozy beer garden. Tours are available Monday to Friday, 10 AM to 4 PM, and cost $10 per person. Booking is recommended and can be done by calling +49 7748 5220. Address: Rothaus 1, 79865 Grafenhausen.

5. Alde Gott Winzer eG, Sasbachwalden: This cooperative winery produces a variety of wines, including Riesling and Pinot Gris. The winery offers tastings and tours that provide insight into the winemaking process. Tastings cost around $10-15 and are available Monday to Saturday, 10 AM to 5 PM. Reservations can be made by calling +49 7841 64070. Address: Talstraße 2, 77887 Sasbachwalden.

6. Weingut Andreas Männle, Durbach: This family-run winery is known for its high-quality wines, including Spätburgunder and Riesling. The winery offers tastings by appointment, with prices starting at $15 per person. The tasting room is open Monday to Saturday, 10 AM to 6 PM. Reservations can be made by calling +49 781 42181. Address: Rebstockweg 9, 77770 Durbach.

Tips for Enjoying Local Cuisine and Dining

- Timing Your Meals: In Germany, lunch is the main meal of the day and is typically served between 12 PM and 2 PM. Dinner is usually lighter and served from 6 PM to 8 PM. Many restaurants close in the afternoon between lunch and dinner services, so plan your meals accordingly.
- Reservations: It's advisable to make reservations, especially for dinner and at popular restaurants, to ensure you get a table. This is particularly important for Michelin-starred restaurants and during weekends.
- Cash vs. Card: While many establishments accept credit cards, some smaller restaurants and cafes may only take cash. It's a good idea to carry some euros with you, especially when visiting rural areas.
- Tipping: In Germany, a tip of around 5-10% is customary for good service. You can either round up the bill or leave a few extra euros on the table.
- Dietary Preferences: Most restaurants will accommodate dietary restrictions if informed in advance. Vegetarian and vegan options are becoming more common, and many places will have gluten-free dishes available.
- Local Markets: For a truly authentic experience, visit local markets where you can sample fresh produce, artisanal cheeses, sausages, and other regional specialties. The weekly market in Freiburg, held on Münsterplatz every Wednesday and Saturday, is a great place to start.

CHAPTER SIX
ACCOMMODATION

6.1 Types of Accommodation

6.1.1 Hotels and Resorts

The Black Forest region offers a wide array of hotels and resorts that cater to different tastes and budgets. Whether you're looking for a luxurious retreat or a cozy, family-friendly place to stay, there's something for everyone.

Luxury Hotels

Luxury hotels in the Black Forest often feature opulent amenities such as spa facilities, gourmet restaurants, and stunning views of the surrounding landscape. The Brenners Park-Hotel & Spa in Baden-Baden is a prime example. Located at Schillerstraße 4/6, 76530 Baden-Baden, this five-star hotel boasts a world-class spa, Michelin-starred dining, and beautifully appointed rooms with an average nightly rate of $400. Guests can indulge in a variety of wellness treatments, take a dip in the indoor pool, or simply relax in the elegant surroundings.

Another top luxury option is the Hotel Traube Tonbach in Baiersbronn. This historic hotel, located at Tonbachstraße 237, 72270 Baiersbronn, has been welcoming guests since 1789. It features several gourmet restaurants, including the three-star Michelin restaurant Schwarzwaldstube. Rooms here start at around $350 per night. The hotel offers a range of activities, from guided hikes to cooking classes, ensuring guests have a memorable stay.

Mid-Range Hotels

For those seeking comfort without breaking the bank, mid-range hotels like the Park Hotel Post in Freiburg provide an excellent balance of quality and affordability. Located at Eisenbahnstraße 35-37, 79098 Freiburg, this charming hotel offers comfortable rooms with modern amenities for around $150 per night. Guests can enjoy a complimentary breakfast, free Wi-Fi, and easy access to the city's attractions.

The Hotel Ritter Durbach, situated at Tal 1, 77770 Durbach, is another great mid-range option. This four-star hotel combines historical charm with contemporary comforts, offering rooms starting at $170 per night. The hotel features a spa, an indoor pool, and an excellent restaurant serving regional specialties.

Budget Hotels

Travelers on a budget will find plenty of affordable options in the Black Forest. The Black Forest Hostel in Freiburg offers dormitory-style accommodation starting at $25 per night. Located at Kartäuserstraße 33, 79102 Freiburg, the hostel is within walking distance of many of the city's attractions. It provides a communal kitchen, free Wi-Fi, and bike rentals, making it a convenient base for exploring the area.

In Baden-Baden, the Hotel Am Friedrichsbad, located at Gernsbacher Str. 31, 76530 Baden-Baden, offers budget-friendly rooms starting at $80 per night. This simple yet comfortable hotel is perfect for travelers who want to enjoy the town's famous thermal baths without spending a fortune.

6.1.2 Bed and Breakfasts

Bed and breakfasts (B&Bs) are a popular choice for travelers looking for a more intimate and personalized experience.

The Black Forest is home to numerous charming B&Bs, often run by local families who provide a warm welcome and insider tips.

The Gästehaus Gerda in Seebach is a delightful B&B located at Grimmerswaldstraße 10, 77889 Seebach. With rooms starting at $90 per night, guests can enjoy a hearty homemade breakfast, comfortable accommodations, and stunning views of the surrounding countryside. The B&B is a perfect base for hiking and exploring the nearby Mummelsee.

In the quaint village of Hinterzarten, the Landhaus Langeck, located at Am Sommerberg 1, 79856 Hinterzarten, offers cozy rooms starting at $100 per night. This family-run B&B features traditional decor, a delicious breakfast, and a peaceful garden where guests can unwind after a day of exploring.

6.1.3 Vacation Rentals

For those who prefer the comfort and convenience of a home away from home, vacation rentals are an excellent option. From charming cottages to modern apartments, there are plenty of choices to suit different needs and preferences.

Airbnb offers a wide range of vacation rentals throughout the Black Forest. For example, a traditional Black Forest house in the village of Sasbachwalden can be rented for around $150 per night. This spacious house, complete with a fully equipped kitchen, fireplace, and stunning mountain views, is perfect for families or groups.

In Freiburg, a modern apartment in the heart of the city can be rented for around $120 per night. Located within walking distance of the main attractions, this stylish apartment offers all the amenities you need for a comfortable stay, including free Wi-Fi, a well-equipped kitchen, and a cozy living area.

6.2 Top Recommendations

6.2.1 *Luxury Stays*

1. Brenners Park-Hotel & Spa, Baden-Baden

Brenners Park-Hotel & Spa is a historic five-star hotel located in the heart of Baden-Baden. Renowned for its elegance, world-class service, and luxurious amenities, it offers a quintessential Black Forest experience. The hotel is part of the Oetker Collection, known for its unique and prestigious properties.

- Address: Schillerstraße 4/6, 76530 Baden-Baden

Amenities:

- Spa and wellness center with indoor pool, sauna, and various treatments
- Michelin-starred restaurant, Brenners Park-Restaurant
- Beautifully landscaped gardens
- Elegant rooms and suites with modern amenities
- Fitness center
- Library and business center

Average Cost:

- Rooms start at approximately $400 per night, with suites and premium accommodations costing significantly more.

2. Hotel Traube Tonbach, Baiersbronn

Hotel Traube Tonbach is a family-run luxury hotel situated in Baiersbronn, a town famous for its culinary excellence.

With a history dating back to 1789, the hotel combines traditional charm with modern luxury, offering an exceptional stay in the Black Forest.

- Address: Tonbachstraße 237, 72270 Baiersbronn

Amenities:

- Several gourmet restaurants, including the three-Michelin-starred Schwarzwaldstube
- Extensive wellness area with indoor and outdoor pools, saunas, and a variety of treatments
- Luxurious rooms and suites with stunning views of the Black Forest
- Fitness center and sports facilities
- Children's programs and family-friendly activities

Average Cost:

- Rooms start at around $350 per night, with suites and exclusive packages available at higher rates.

3. Hotel Bareiss, Baiersbronn

Hotel Bareiss is another gem in Baiersbronn, offering a blend of luxury, tradition, and hospitality. This five-star hotel is known for its exceptional service, gourmet dining, and comprehensive wellness facilities.

- Address: Hermine-Bareiss-Weg, 72270 Baiersbronn

Amenities:

- Multiple gourmet restaurants, including the three-Michelin-starred Restaurant Bareiss
- Extensive spa and wellness area with pools, saunas, and treatment rooms
- Luxurious rooms and suites with elegant decor

- Fitness center and outdoor sports facilities
- Children's club and family activities
- Private forest for walks and picnics

Average Cost:

- Rooms start at approximately $380 per night, with higher rates for suites and special packages.

4. Parkhotel Adler, Hinterzarten

Parkhotel Adler is a historic luxury hotel in Hinterzarten, offering a blend of tradition and modernity. Surrounded by beautiful parkland, this family-run hotel provides a serene and elegant escape in the Black Forest.

- Address: Adlerweg 23, 79856 Hinterzarten

Amenities:

- Spa and wellness area with indoor and outdoor pools, saunas, and treatment rooms
- Fine dining restaurant and cozy bistro
- Luxurious rooms and suites with traditional and contemporary decor
- Fitness center and sports facilities
- Private park with walking paths and outdoor activities
- Children's programs and family-friendly services

Average Cost:

- Rooms start at around $300 per night, with higher rates for suites and special packages.

5. Hotel Dollenberg, Bad Peterstal-Griesbach

Hotel Dollenberg is a luxurious spa hotel located in Bad Peterstal-Griesbach. Known for its breathtaking views and exceptional wellness facilities, it is an ideal destination for relaxation and rejuvenation.

- Address: Dollenberg 3, 77740 Bad Peterstal-Griesbach

Amenities:

- Extensive spa and wellness area with multiple pools, saunas, and treatment rooms
- Gourmet restaurant, Le Pavillon, awarded with two Michelin stars
- Luxurious rooms and suites with panoramic views
- Fitness center and outdoor sports facilities
- Beautiful gardens and parkland
- Entertainment programs and live music

Average Cost:

- Rooms start at approximately $350 per night, with higher rates for suites and special packages.

6.2.2 Budget-Friendly Options

1. Black Forest Hostel, Freiburg

- Address: Kartäuserstraße 33, 79102 Freiburg

Located in the vibrant city of Freiburg, the Black Forest Hostel is an excellent choice for budget-conscious travelers seeking a comfortable and friendly atmosphere. This hostel offers dormitory-style accommodation and private rooms, catering to solo travelers, groups, and families.

Rates:

- Dormitory beds: starting at $25 per night
- Private rooms: starting at $60 per night

Amenities:

- Free Wi-Fi
- Communal kitchen
- Bicycle rentals
- Common lounge area
- Laundry facilities

Tips:

Take advantage of the hostel's bike rental service to explore Freiburg and its surroundings. The hostel's central location makes it easy to visit local attractions such as the Freiburg Minster and the Schlossberg hill. Join the hostel's social events to meet other travelers and share experiences.

2. Hotel Etol, Baden-Baden

- Address: Merkelstraße 4, 76530 Baden-Baden

Situated in the heart of Baden-Baden, Hotel Etol offers budget-friendly rooms with a touch of elegance. This charming hotel is just a short walk from the town's famous thermal baths, making it an ideal base for exploring the area.

Rates:

- Rooms: starting at $75 per night

Amenities:

- Free Wi-Fi
- Complimentary breakfast
- En-suite bathrooms
- Cable TV
- Garden terrace

Tips:

Enjoy a leisurely breakfast in the hotel's garden terrace before heading out to explore Baden-Baden. The Caracalla Spa and Friedrichsbad are within walking distance, providing a relaxing experience without the high cost. Ask the friendly staff for recommendations on affordable dining options in the area.

3. Gasthof Hotel zum Wasserfall, Triberg

- Address: Hauptstraße 19, 78098 Triberg

Located in the picturesque town of Triberg, famous for its waterfalls and cuckoo clocks, Gasthof Hotel zum Wasserfall offers affordable accommodation with a traditional Black Forest charm. This family-run guesthouse provides a warm and welcoming atmosphere.

Rates:

- Rooms: starting at $65 per night

Amenities:

- Free Wi-Fi
- Complimentary breakfast
- Restaurant serving regional cuisine
- Free parking
- Terrace with waterfall views

Tips:

Take a short walk to the Triberg Waterfalls, one of the highest waterfalls in Germany. The hotel's restaurant offers delicious regional dishes at reasonable prices. Visit the Black Forest Museum nearby to learn more about the area's history and culture.

4. Pension Williams, Seebach

- Address: Ruhesteinstraße 67, 77889 Seebach

Nestled in the heart of the Black Forest, Pension Williams is a budget-friendly guesthouse offering cozy rooms and stunning views of the surrounding countryside. This family-run B&B is perfect for nature lovers and outdoor enthusiasts.

Rates:

- Rooms: starting at $60 per night

Amenities:

- Free Wi-Fi
- Complimentary breakfast
- En-suite bathrooms
- Common lounge area
- Hiking trail access

Tips:

Use the guesthouse as a base for exploring the nearby Mummelsee and hiking the surrounding trails. The owners are knowledgeable about the area and can provide great recommendations for outdoor activities and local attractions. Enjoy a hearty homemade breakfast before heading out for the day.

5. Jugendherberge Titisee-Neustadt

- Address: Schildwende 20, 79822 Titisee-Neustadt

This youth hostel in Titisee-Neustadt offers budget-friendly accommodation in a scenic setting near Lake Titisee. Ideal for families, groups, and solo travelers, the hostel provides a range of amenities and activities.

Rates:

- Dormitory beds: starting at $30 per night
- Private rooms: starting at $70 per night

Amenities:

- Free Wi-Fi
- Complimentary breakfast
- Family rooms
- Outdoor playground
- Sports facilities

Tips:

Enjoy the hostel's sports facilities, including basketball and volleyball courts, and explore the nearby Lake Titisee for swimming and boating. The hostel organizes various activities and excursions, making it a fun and engaging place to stay. Book early to secure the best rates, especially during peak travel seasons.

By choosing these budget-friendly accommodations, you can enjoy the beauty and charm of the Black Forest without straining your wallet.

6.2.3 Unique Places to Stay

The Black Forest offers a variety of unique accommodations that provide not only comfort but also a memorable and distinctive experience. Here are some top recommendations for unique places to stay in the region:

1. Baumhaushotel Schwarzwald (Treehouse Hotel)

For a magical experience, consider staying at the Baumhaushotel Schwarzwald. This treehouse hotel offers the chance to sleep among the treetops, surrounded by the tranquil beauty of the Black Forest.

- Location: Tannenweg 1, 75378 Bad Wildbad
- Amenities: Each treehouse is equipped with modern amenities, including a private bathroom, cozy sitting area, heating, and a balcony with forest views.
- Activities: The hotel is located near the Baumwipfelpfad (Treetop Walk), providing guests with unique opportunities for hiking and exploring the forest canopy.
- Rates: Starting at $180 per night.

2. Hotel Saigerhöh

Situated at a high altitude, the Hotel Saigerhöh offers panoramic views of the Black Forest, luxurious rooms, and a wellness area that ensures a relaxing stay.

- Location: Saiger Höhe 8-10, 79853 Lenzkirch
- Amenities: The hotel features an indoor pool, sauna, spa services, a restaurant serving regional cuisine, and spacious rooms with modern decor.
- Activities: Guests can enjoy guided hiking tours, culinary workshops, and access to nearby trails for both summer and winter activities.
- Rates: Starting at $200 per night.

3. Vogtsbauernhof Open-Air Museum Stays

Experience living history by staying in traditional Black Forest farmhouses at the Vogtsbauernhof Open-Air Museum. These historic houses offer a unique glimpse into the region's past.

- Location: Wählerbrücke 1, 77793 Gutach

- Amenities: Authentic historical furnishings, rustic charm, guided tours of the museum, and participation in traditional crafts and activities.
- Activities: Explore the open-air museum, participate in workshops, and enjoy themed events that bring history to life.
- Rates: Starting at $160 per night.

4. Das Schäferwagen Hotel (Shepherd's Wagon Hotel)

For a unique and cozy experience, stay at Das Schäferwagen Hotel, where guests can sleep in beautifully restored shepherd's wagons.

- Location: Kinzigtalstraße 20, 77784 Oberharmersbach
- Amenities: Each wagon is equipped with a comfortable bed, heating, a small kitchenette, and a seating area. Bathrooms are shared but modern and well-maintained.
- Activities: The hotel offers bike rentals, hiking trails, and is close to local attractions such as the Harmersbacher Vesperweg.
- Rates: Starting at $140 per night.

5. Berggasthof Präger Böden (Mountain Inn)

Nestled high in the Black Forest mountains, Berggasthof Präger Böden offers an idyllic escape with stunning views and a rustic atmosphere.

- Location: Präger Böden 1, 79674 Todtnau
- Amenities: Comfortable rooms with mountain views, a restaurant serving local cuisine, and a sun terrace.
- Activities: The inn is a perfect base for hiking, skiing in winter, and exploring the nearby Feldberg mountain.

- Rates: Starting at $130 per night.

6. Schluchsee Floating Houses

For an extraordinary stay, book a floating house on Lake Schluchsee. These unique accommodations offer stunning lake views and direct access to water activities.

- Location: Am Schluchsee 3, 79859 Schluchsee
- Amenities: Modern, well-equipped floating houses with private terraces, kitchens, and cozy living areas.
- Activities: Enjoy swimming, kayaking, fishing, and scenic boat rides directly from your doorstep.
- Rates: Starting at $250 per night.

7. Klosterhof St. Blasien (Monastery Stay)

Immerse yourself in tranquility and history by staying at the Klosterhof in St. Blasien. This former monastery offers a serene environment with a touch of historical charm.

- Location: Klosterstraße 2, 79837 St. Blasien
- Amenities: Simple yet comfortable rooms, beautiful gardens, a library, and a meditation room.
- Activities: Participate in meditation sessions, explore the historic monastery, and enjoy the peaceful surroundings.
- Rates: Starting at $110 per night.

Each of these unique accommodations offers an unforgettable experience, blending the natural beauty of the Black Forest with the rich cultural heritage of the region.

6.3 Booking Tips
1. Best Websites

When booking accommodation in the Black Forest, several websites offer reliable options and great deals. Booking.com is a popular choice, offering a wide range of hotels, B&Bs, and vacation rentals with user reviews and competitive prices. Airbnb is ideal for finding unique vacation rentals, such as cottages and apartments, often with a local touch.

Another excellent resource is the official Black Forest tourism website (www.blackforest-tourism.com), which provides comprehensive information on accommodation, including special offers and packages.

2. Timing and Discounts

Booking your accommodation well in advance, especially during peak travel seasons, can help secure the best rates and availability. Consider traveling during the shoulder seasons (spring and autumn) when the weather is pleasant, and prices are lower.

Many hotels and B&Bs offer discounts for extended stays or last-minute bookings. Signing up for newsletters from your preferred booking sites can also alert you to special deals and promotions. Additionally, using travel rewards points or loyalty programs can result in significant savings.

For those planning to stay in multiple locations within the Black Forest, consider booking a combination of different types of accommodation to experience the region fully. This approach allows you to enjoy the luxury of a high-end hotel for a few nights and then switch to a cozy B&B or a unique vacation rental for a different perspective.

By carefully selecting your accommodation and taking advantage of available discounts and booking tips, you can ensure a comfortable and memorable stay in the beautiful Black Forest.

CHAPTER SEVEN
SHOPPING AND SOUVENIRS

7.1 Local Markets

7.1.1 What to Buy

Shopping in the Black Forest is an adventure in itself, offering a treasure trove of unique items and traditional crafts that make for perfect souvenirs and gifts. Here's a detailed look at what you should consider buying:

1. Cuckoo Clocks: The quintessential Black Forest souvenir, cuckoo clocks have been crafted in this region for centuries. These clocks are renowned for their intricate designs and precise craftsmanship. Traditional cuckoo clocks often feature detailed carvings of forest scenes, wildlife, and traditional Black Forest houses. Some modern designs incorporate contemporary elements while still maintaining the classic charm. Prices vary widely; you can find simple designs for around $50, but more elaborate, hand-carved clocks can cost upwards of $1,000. A great place to start your search is the House of 1000 Clocks in Triberg, where you can explore a vast collection of these beautiful timepieces.

2. Wooden Toys and Carvings: The Black Forest is famous for its woodcraft, and you'll find an array of wooden toys and carvings in the local markets. Artisans create everything from simple children's toys to intricate sculptures. Popular items include wooden animals, puzzles, and detailed figurines. Small items can cost as little as $10, while larger, more detailed carvings can be priced up to $200. The Black Forest Woodcarving Museum in Triberg offers both a fascinating look at the history of woodcarving and a shop where you can purchase these exquisite items.

3. Glassware: Another notable craft from the Black Forest is hand-blown glass. The Dorotheenhütte Glassworks in Wolfach is an excellent place to witness the glassblowing process and purchase unique glass ornaments, vases, and other decorative items. Prices range from $20 for smaller pieces to $150 for more elaborate designs. You can even try your hand at glassblowing, creating a personalized souvenir to take home.

4. Local Wines and Spirits: The Black Forest region, particularly the Baden wine area, is known for its high-quality wines. Riesling and Pinot Noir are among the most popular varieties. Prices for a good bottle of local wine typically range from $15 to $50. Additionally, the Black Forest is famous for its Schnapps, a traditional German spirit often infused with local fruits and herbs. A bottle of Schnapps makes a delightful gift, with prices starting at around $20.

5. Black Forest Ham: No visit to the Black Forest is complete without sampling the famous Black Forest ham. This smoked delicacy, known for its distinctive flavor, is a perfect souvenir for food enthusiasts. You can purchase vacuum-sealed packs that are easy to transport. Prices are around $20 per pound. Look for authentic Black Forest ham at local markets or specialty shops like the Edeka supermarkets in Freiburg.

6. Bollenhut Hats: These traditional hats, adorned with red or black pom-poms, are a symbol of the Black Forest. While they are primarily worn during cultural festivals, miniature versions make charming souvenirs. Prices for these hats are typically around $30. They are available at various local markets and specialty shops throughout the region.

7.1.2 Best Markets to Visit

1. Freiburg Münster Market: Located in the heart of Freiburg, this market is held every day except Sundays around the iconic Freiburg Minster. It's one of the largest and most vibrant markets in the Black Forest, offering a mix of fresh produce, flowers, and local crafts. You'll find stalls selling everything from handmade candles and soaps to wooden toys and leather goods. The market is also a fantastic place to sample local foods, including freshly baked bread, cheeses, and Black Forest ham. Open from 7:30 AM to 1:30 PM, it's best visited in the morning when the selection is at its best. Address: Münsterplatz, 79098 Freiburg im Breisgau, Germany.

2. Offenburg Farmer's Market: One of the oldest markets in the region, the Offenburg Farmer's Market is held on Tuesdays, Thursdays, and Saturdays. It's a lively market offering a wide range of local products, including cheeses, meats, fruits, and vegetables. You'll also find stalls selling flowers, honey, and handcrafted items. It's an excellent place to experience the local culture and taste regional specialties. The market is open from 8:00 AM to 1:00 PM and is located at Marktplatz, 77652 Offenburg, Germany.

3. Baden-Baden Christmas Market: If you're visiting the Black Forest during the holiday season, the Baden-Baden Christmas Market is a must-visit. This festive market runs from late November to December 30 and offers a magical atmosphere with twinkling lights, festive decorations, and a wide variety of stalls selling Christmas ornaments, handcrafted gifts, and delicious treats. Be sure to try the Glühwein (mulled wine) and traditional German Christmas cookies. The market is open daily from 11:00 AM to 9:00 PM, making it perfect for evening visits. Address: Kaiserallee, 76530 Baden-Baden, Germany.

4. Triberg Market: Known for its proximity to the Triberg Waterfalls, this market operates on Saturdays and features a variety of local crafts, including cuckoo clocks and wooden carvings. It's smaller than some of the other markets but offers a more intimate shopping experience. You can find a range of traditional Black Forest products, from homemade jams and jellies to intricately carved wooden figures. The market is open from 8:00 AM to 1:00 PM and is located in the town center of Triberg. Address: Hauptstraße, 78098 Triberg im Schwarzwald, Germany.

5. Gengenbach Christmas Market: Another wonderful Christmas market in the Black Forest is in Gengenbach. This market is famous for its Advent calendar, where the windows of the town hall are transformed into a giant Advent calendar, with a new window being opened each day. The market features a variety of stalls selling Christmas decorations, handmade crafts, and local foods. It's open from late November until Christmas Eve, with hours from 2:00 PM to 8:00 PM on weekdays and from 12:00 PM to 8:00 PM on weekends. Address: Marktplatz, 77723 Gengenbach, Germany.

6. Villingen-Schwenningen Market: This market is held twice a week, on Wednesdays and Saturdays, in the historic town of Villingen-Schwenningen. It offers a wide range of fresh produce, meats, cheeses, and baked goods, as well as flowers and handcrafted items. The market is a great place to mingle with locals and enjoy the vibrant atmosphere. Open from 7:00 AM to 12:30 PM, it's best visited in the morning. Address: Münsterplatz, 78050 Villingen-Schwenningen, Germany.

7. Donaueschingen Market: Held on Tuesdays and Fridays, this market offers a variety of local products, including fresh

fruits and vegetables, meats, cheeses, and baked goods. You'll also find stalls selling flowers, plants, and handcrafted items. The market is open from 8:00 AM to 1:00 PM and is located in the town center of Donaueschingen. Address: Karlstraße, 78166 Donaueschingen, Germany.

8. Calw Market: Located in the picturesque town of Calw, this market is held on Saturdays and offers a range of local products, including fresh produce, meats, cheeses, and baked goods. You'll also find stalls selling flowers, plants, and handcrafted items. The market is open from 8:00 AM to 1:00 PM and is located in the town center of Calw. Address: Marktplatz, 75365 Calw, Germany.

9. Baiersbronn Farmer's Market: This market is held on Thursdays and offers a variety of local products, including fresh produce, meats, cheeses, and baked goods. You'll also find stalls selling flowers, plants, and handcrafted items. The market is open from 8:00 AM to 1:00 PM and is located in the town center of Baiersbronn. Address: Rosenplatz, 72270 Baiersbronn, Germany.

10. Titisee Market: Held on Wednesdays, this market offers a variety of local products, including fresh produce, meats, cheeses, and baked goods. You'll also find stalls selling flowers, plants, and handcrafted items. The market is open from 8:00 AM to 1:00 PM and is located in the town center of Titisee. Address: Seestraße, 79822 Titisee-Neustadt, Germany.

11. Schiltach Market: This market is held on Fridays and offers a variety of local products, including fresh produce, meats, cheeses, and baked goods. You'll also find stalls selling flowers, plants, and handcrafted items. The market is open from 8:00 AM to 1:00 PM and is located in the town

center of Schiltach. Address: Marktplatz, 77761 Schiltach, Germany.

Each of these markets offers a unique shopping experience, allowing you to immerse yourself in the local culture and find one-of-a-kind souvenirs.

7.2 Specialty Shops
7.2.1 Cuckoo Clocks

Cuckoo clocks are arguably the most iconic souvenirs from the Black Forest. The region is the birthplace of these charming timepieces, renowned for their craftsmanship and intricate designs. Here are some of the best places to purchase an authentic Black Forest cuckoo clock.

1. House of 1000 Clocks (Haus der 1000 Uhren)

Located in Triberg, the House of 1000 Clocks is a must-visit for anyone looking to buy a cuckoo clock. This shop offers an extensive range of clocks, from traditional chalet styles to modern designs. Each clock is handcrafted with meticulous detail, ensuring that every piece is unique. Prices start at around $50 for simpler designs and can go up to several thousand dollars for more elaborate models.

- Address: Hauptstraße 79-81, 78098 Triberg im Schwarzwald, Germany
- Opening Hours: Monday to Saturday, 10:00 AM - 6:00 PM; Sunday, 11:00 AM - 5:00 PM

2. Hubert Herr Cuckoo Clocks

This family-run business in Triberg has been producing cuckoo clocks for over 150 years. Hubert Herr is known for their high-quality clocks that blend traditional craftsmanship with innovative designs. Their clocks range from classic to contemporary styles, catering to a wide array of tastes.

- Address: Schonachbach 27, 78098 Triberg, Germany
- Opening Hours: Monday to Friday, 9:00 AM - 5:00 PM; Saturday, 10:00 AM - 2:00 PM

3. Hönes Cuckoo Clocks

Located in Titisee-Neustadt, Hönes is another prominent name in the cuckoo clock industry. Their clocks are renowned for their innovative mechanisms and exquisite craftsmanship. Hönes offers a variety of styles, from the deeply traditional to the sleek and modern, ensuring there is something for everyone.

- Address: Jostalstraße 60, 79822 Titisee-Neustadt, Germany
- Opening Hours: Monday to Friday, 8:00 AM - 5:00 PM

7.2.2 Handcrafted Goods

In addition to cuckoo clocks, the Black Forest is home to many artisans who create a wide variety of handcrafted goods. From wooden carvings to blown glass, these items make perfect souvenirs and gifts.

1. Black Forest Woodcarving Museum (Schwarzwaldmuseum)

Located in Triberg, the Black Forest Woodcarving Museum showcases the rich tradition of woodcarving in the region. The museum also features a shop where visitors can purchase finely crafted wooden items. These range from small figurines to larger decorative pieces, each intricately carved by local artisans.

- Address: Wallfahrtstraße 4, 78098 Triberg, Germany
- Opening Hours: Monday to Sunday, 10:00 AM - 5:00 PM

2. Dorotheenhütte Glassworks

In Wolfach, the Dorotheenhütte Glassworks is the last remaining glassworks in the Black Forest where visitors can watch glassblowers at work. The shop offers a variety of hand-blown glass items, including ornaments, vases, and decorative pieces. Prices for glass items range from $20 to $150, depending on the size and complexity.

- Address: Glashüttenweg 4, 77709 Wolfach, Germany
- Opening Hours: Monday to Sunday, 9:00 AM - 5:00 PM

3. Vogtsbauernhof Open-Air Museum

The Vogtsbauernhof Open-Air Museum in Gutach not only showcases traditional Black Forest farmhouses but also features a shop selling handmade crafts and local produce. This is an excellent place to find unique souvenirs that reflect the region's cultural heritage.

- Address: Vogtsbauernhof 1, 77793 Gutach, Germany
- Opening Hours: Monday to Sunday, 9:00 AM - 6:00 PM

7.3 Shopping Tips
Bargaining

While bargaining is not as common in Germany as it is in some other countries, there are still opportunities to negotiate, especially at markets and with small vendors.

- Do Your Research: Before making a purchase, it's a good idea to check the prices of similar items at different stalls or shops. This gives you a better understanding of the average cost and helps in negotiating a fair price.
- Be Polite: Approach bargaining with a friendly and respectful attitude. Start by asking if the seller can offer a discount, and be prepared to make a reasonable counteroffer.
- Cash is King: Vendors are often more willing to offer discounts for cash payments, as it saves them credit card processing fees. Always carry some cash when shopping at markets and smaller shops.
- Bundle Purchases: If you're buying multiple items from the same vendor, ask for a discount on the total price. Vendors are more likely to offer a better deal for larger purchases.
- End-of-Day Discounts: Visit markets towards the end of the day when vendors are more inclined to lower prices to sell off their remaining stock.

Tax-Free Shopping

Non-EU residents can enjoy tax-free shopping in Germany, allowing them to claim back the VAT (Value Added Tax) on their purchases.

- Minimum Purchase Amount: To qualify for a VAT refund, your purchases from a single store must exceed a certain amount, usually around €25-50 ($30-60). Ask the store for a Tax-Free form when you make your purchase.
- Fill Out the Forms: Ensure that the Tax-Free form is correctly filled out by the retailer, including details of the purchase, the VAT amount, and the store's stamp.

- Keep Receipts: Always keep your original receipts and the Tax-Free forms together, as you'll need to present them at the airport.
- Customs Validation: Before checking in for your flight, present your purchases, receipts, and Tax-Free forms to the customs office at the airport for validation. Ensure that the items are unused and in their original packaging.
- Claim Your Refund: After customs validation, proceed to the Tax-Free refund counter or use a Tax-Free kiosk to get your refund. Refunds can be processed in cash, credited to your credit card, or sent via bank transfer.

CHAPTER EIGHT
HEALTH AND WELLNESS
8.1 Spa and Wellness Retreats
8.1.1 Top Spas
1. Friedrichsbad, Baden-Baden

Friedrichsbad is not just a spa; it is a journey back in time. This historic Roman-Irish bath, built in 1877, combines the best of both bathing traditions in a 17-step ritual that promises to leave you feeling rejuvenated and refreshed. As you step into the grandiose bathhouse, you are greeted by an atmosphere of old-world charm and tranquility.

The 17-Step Ritual

- Warm Shower: Begin with a thorough shower to cleanse the body.
- Warm Air Bath: Relax in a room with a temperature of around 54°C (129°F), allowing your body to acclimate to the heat.
- Hot Air Bath: Move to a hotter room, heated to approximately 68°C (154°F), to open pores and begin the detoxification process.
- Thermal Steam Bath: Enjoy a steam bath infused with thermal waters to further cleanse the skin and promote relaxation.
- Hot Thermal Pool: Immerse yourself in a hot thermal pool, where the mineral-rich waters help to soothe muscles and joints.
- Soap and Brush Massage: Experience a vigorous soap and brush massage, which exfoliates the skin and stimulates circulation.

- Thermal Inhalation: Breathe in the therapeutic steam to clear respiratory pathways and enhance well-being.
- Cold Plunge Pool: Take a brief dip in a cold plunge pool to invigorate the body and close the pores.
- Warm Thermal Pool: Return to a warmer pool to stabilize your body temperature and relax.
- Warm Air Bath: Relax once again in a warm air bath to gradually cool down.
- Moisturizing Cream Application: Apply moisturizing cream to nourish the skin.
- Rest and Relaxation: Spend time in the relaxation area, allowing your body to absorb the benefits of the treatments.

Average Cost: The full 17-step ritual costs approximately $50. A simplified package, excluding the soap and brush massage, is available for around $35.

- Opening Hours: Monday to Sunday: 9:00 AM - 10:00 PM
- Location and Contact: Römerplatz 1, 76530 Baden-Baden, Germany.

2. Caracalla Spa, Baden-Baden

Located in the same town, Caracalla Spa offers a more modern wellness experience. This expansive spa spans over 43,000 square feet and features indoor and outdoor thermal pools, saunas, and various wellness treatments. The spa's thermal waters, sourced from a depth of 6,500 feet, are renowned for their healing properties.

Facilities and Treatments

- Thermal Pools: Caracalla Spa boasts numerous thermal pools with temperatures ranging from 32°C

to 38°C (90°F to 100°F). These pools are rich in minerals that are beneficial for the skin and overall health.
- Sauna Area: The extensive sauna area includes a variety of saunas, from a traditional Finnish sauna to a more unique aromatic steam bath. The sauna garden, with its beautiful landscaping, offers a serene space to relax between sessions.
- Wellness Treatments: Caracalla Spa offers a range of wellness treatments, including massages, facials, and body wraps. The spa's professional therapists use high-quality products to ensure a luxurious experience.
- Average Cost: A two-hour session costs around $25, while a full day pass is approximately $40. Special packages, including sauna access, start at $50.
- Opening Hours: Monday to Sunday: 8:00 AM - 10:00 PM
- Location and Contact: Römerplatz 1, 76530 Baden-Baden, Germany.

3. Palais Thermal, Bad Wildbad

Palais Thermal, located in Bad Wildbad, is renowned for its luxurious ambiance and historic charm. This spa is housed in an elegant building that dates back to the 19th century, offering a unique blend of classical architecture and modern wellness facilities.

Highlights of Palais Thermal

- Thermal Baths: The thermal baths at Palais Thermal are filled with mineral-rich waters that have been renowned for their healing properties for centuries.

The baths are set in beautifully decorated rooms that enhance the overall experience.
- Sauna Area: The sauna area at Palais Thermal includes various types of saunas and steam baths. The rooftop terrace offers stunning views of the Black Forest, making it a perfect place to relax and unwind.
- Spa Treatments: Guests can choose from a variety of treatments, including massages, facials, and body treatments. The spa's professional therapists use premium products and techniques to ensure a relaxing and rejuvenating experience.
- Average Cost: The "Wellness Deluxe" package, which includes access to all thermal baths, saunas, and a choice of two 30-minute treatments, costs approximately $150 per day.
- Opening Hours: Monday to Sunday: 9:00 AM - 10:00 PM
- Location and Contact: Kernerstraße 5, 75323 Bad Wildbad, Germany.

4. Brenners Park-Hotel & Spa, Baden-Baden

Brenners Park-Hotel & Spa is synonymous with luxury and elegance. This five-star hotel offers a range of wellness packages designed to rejuvenate the body and mind. The spa facilities are state-of-the-art, and the holistic approach ensures a comprehensive wellness experience.

Signature Wellness Packages

- The King's Way: This package includes personalized wellness consultations, spa treatments, and gourmet healthy meals. Guests can enjoy tailored massages, hydrotherapy sessions, and beauty treatments.

- Detox and Rejuvenation: Focused on detoxifying the body, this package includes detoxifying treatments, a personalized diet plan, and fitness sessions.
- Mind and Body Balance: Aimed at achieving harmony between mind and body, this package includes yoga sessions, meditation classes, and stress-relief treatments.
- Average Cost: The "King's Way" package starts at $500 per day, including accommodation, treatments, and meals.
- Amenities: The hotel features an indoor pool, fitness center, and gourmet restaurant, all designed to enhance the wellness experience.
- Location and Contact: Schillerstraße 4/6, 76530 Baden-Baden, Germany.

8.1.2 Wellness Packages

1. Thermalbad Überlingen, Überlingen

Located on the shores of Lake Constance, Thermalbad Überlingen offers a serene and picturesque setting for a wellness retreat. The spa features indoor and outdoor thermal pools, saunas, and a range of wellness treatments designed to promote relaxation and well-being.

Wellness Packages

- Lake View Relaxation: This package includes access to all thermal pools, a 60-minute full-body massage, and a detoxifying body wrap. Guests can enjoy stunning views of Lake Constance while indulging in the spa's luxurious facilities.
- Thermal Healing: Focused on the therapeutic properties of thermal water, this package includes

hydrotherapy sessions, thermal steam baths, and a personalized health consultation.
- Pamper Day: Aimed at providing a day of pure indulgence, this package includes access to all spa facilities, a 30-minute facial, a 60-minute massage, and a gourmet lunch at the spa's restaurant.
- Average Cost: The "Lake View Relaxation" package costs approximately $120 per day.
- Opening Hours: Monday to Sunday: 9:00 AM - 9:00 PM
- Location and Contact: Christophstraße 18, 88662 Überlingen, Germany.

2. Bareiss, Baiersbronn

Bareiss is a family-run luxury resort in Baiersbronn, offering an array of wellness packages that cater to different needs. The resort's spa facilities are extensive, and the treatments are designed to provide a holistic wellness experience.

Wellness Packages

- Ultimate Relaxation: This package includes a 90-minute full-body massage, access to all spa facilities, and a private wellness suite for the day. Guests can also enjoy a healthy three-course meal prepared by the resort's renowned chef.
- Fitness and Wellness: Aimed at those looking to combine fitness with relaxation, this package includes personal training sessions, yoga classes, and a series of massages and body treatments to aid muscle recovery.
- Beauty and Rejuvenation: Focused on skincare and beauty, this package includes facials, anti-aging

treatments, and makeup consultations. The spa uses high-end skincare products to ensure the best results.
- Average Cost: The "Ultimate Relaxation" package costs around $300 per day.
- Opening Hours: Monday to Sunday: 7:00 AM - 9:00 PM
- Location and Contact: Hermine-Bareiss-Weg, 72270 Baiersbronn, Germany.

3. Vitalhotel Grüner Baum, Todtnau

Nestled in the scenic town of Todtnau, Vitalhotel Grüner Baum offers a range of wellness packages in a serene setting. The hotel's spa facilities include thermal baths, saunas, and treatment rooms where guests can enjoy a variety of therapies.

Wellness Packages

- Nature's Embrace: This package includes access to all spa facilities, a 60-minute herbal massage, and a guided nature walk. The emphasis is on reconnecting with nature and enjoying the therapeutic benefits of the natural surroundings.
- Detox and Purify: Focused on cleansing the body, this package includes detoxifying treatments, such as body wraps and hydrotherapy sessions, as well as a personalized detox diet plan.
- Relaxation Retreat: Aimed at providing a peaceful escape, this package includes a 90-minute relaxation massage, access to all spa facilities, and a gourmet dinner featuring healthy, organic ingredients.
- Average Cost: The "Nature's Embrace" package costs around $150 per day.

- Opening Hours: Monday to Sunday: 8:00 AM - 8:00 PM
- Location and Contact: Schauinslandstraße 28, 79674 Todtnau, Germany.

8.2 Medical Services
Hospitals and Clinics

1. Klinikum Mittelbaden, Baden-Baden

Klinikum Mittelbaden is a well-equipped hospital providing comprehensive medical services, including emergency care, surgery, and specialized treatments. The hospital is known for its high standards of patient care and modern facilities.

- Contact Information: Balger Str. 50, 76532 Baden-Baden, Germany.

2. St. Josefskrankenhaus, Freiburg

St. Josefskrankenhaus in Freiburg offers a wide range of medical services, from general medicine to specialized departments like cardiology and orthopedics. The hospital is staffed by experienced professionals dedicated to providing high-quality healthcare.

- Contact Information: Sautierstraße 1, 79104 Freiburg im Breisgau, Germany.

Emergency Numbers

In case of a medical emergency, dial 112 for immediate assistance. This number connects you to emergency medical services, fire, and police.

8.3 Staying Healthy
Travel Health Tips

1. Hydration and Nutrition

Staying hydrated is crucial, especially when engaging in outdoor activities like hiking and cycling. Carry a reusable water bottle and drink plenty of water throughout the day. The Black Forest region offers an abundance of fresh local produce, making it easy to maintain a balanced diet. Indulge in seasonal fruits, vegetables, and local delicacies like Black Forest ham and cherry cake.

2. Sun Protection

The Black Forest's higher elevations can result in stronger UV exposure. Always wear sunscreen with a high SPF, sunglasses, and a hat when spending time outdoors. Reapply sunscreen regularly, especially after swimming or sweating.

3. Physical Preparation

If you plan on hiking or participating in other strenuous activities, ensure you are physically prepared. Engage in regular exercise before your trip to build stamina and strength. Proper footwear is essential for avoiding injuries on uneven terrain.

Local Pharmacies

1. Freiburg Apotheke, Freiburg

Located conveniently in the heart of Freiburg, Freiburg Apotheke offers a wide range of pharmaceutical products, including over-the-counter medications, prescription drugs, and wellness products. The staff is knowledgeable and can provide advice on minor health issues and recommend suitable treatments.

- Opening Hours: Monday to Friday: 8:00 AM - 6:30 PM, Saturday: 9:00 AM - 2:00 PM
- Location and Contact: Bertoldstraße 44, 79098 Freiburg im Breisgau, Germany.

2. Stadt-Apotheke, Baden-Baden

Stadt-Apotheke in Baden-Baden is a trusted pharmacy providing a comprehensive selection of medications and health products. The pharmacy also offers consultation services, ensuring you receive the best care for your health needs.

- Opening Hours: Monday to Friday: 8:00 AM - 6:30 PM, Saturday: 9:00 AM - 1:00 PM
- Location and Contact: Lange Str. 19, 76530 Baden-Baden, Germany. Phone: +49 7221 23560.

With its blend of luxurious spa experiences, top-notch medical services, and practical health tips, the Black Forest region ensures that your well-being is taken care of, allowing you to fully immerse yourself in the natural beauty and cultural richness of this enchanting destination.

CHAPTER NINE
SUSTAINABLE TRAVEL

9.1 Eco-Friendly Practices

1. Green Accommodations

In the heart of the Black Forest, sustainable travel starts with choosing eco-friendly accommodations. Many hotels and guesthouses in the region are committed to reducing their environmental impact through various green practices. One such establishment is the Hotel Schwarzwald Panorama, located at Rehteichweg 22, 75378 Bad Herrenalb. This four-star hotel uses solar panels for energy, implements water-saving technologies, and offers organic meals sourced from local farms. Prices range from $120 to $200 per night, depending on the season and room type.

The Biohotel Rose in Hayingen is another excellent option. This family-run hotel is entirely organic, from the building materials to the food served. Located at Im Dorf 5, 72534 Hayingen, the Biohotel Rose offers rooms starting at $100 per night. Guests can enjoy vegetarian and vegan meals prepared with ingredients from the hotel's own garden. The hotel also provides electric bike rentals for eco-friendly exploration of the surrounding area.

To get the most out of your stay, inquire about any green initiatives the hotel participates in. Many hotels offer tours of their eco-friendly facilities or workshops on sustainable living practices. Also, look for the "Green Key" certification, an international standard for environmentally responsible accommodations.

2. Responsible Hiking and Camping

The Black Forest is a haven for outdoor enthusiasts, with its extensive network of hiking trails and picturesque camping sites. To preserve the natural beauty of the region, it's crucial to follow responsible hiking and camping practices. One of the most popular hiking routes is the Westweg, a long-distance trail stretching over 177 miles from Pforzheim to Basel. While hiking, stick to marked trails to minimize your impact on the environment and avoid disturbing wildlife.

Camping in the Black Forest is a memorable experience, especially in designated campsites that prioritize sustainability. The Campingplatz Kirnbergsee, located at Seestraße 34, 78199 Bräunlingen, offers eco-friendly camping with facilities such as solar-heated showers and recycling stations. Prices for a tent pitch start at $20 per night.

When camping, always adhere to the "Leave No Trace" principles. This means packing out all trash, minimizing campfire impact, and respecting wildlife. Additionally, consider using biodegradable soap and toiletries to reduce your environmental footprint.

9.2 Supporting Local Communities
1. Ethical Souvenir Shopping

Shopping for souvenirs is a delightful part of any trip, but it's essential to support local artisans and businesses while ensuring your purchases are ethically made. In the Black Forest, you'll find a plethora of traditional crafts that make perfect souvenirs. One notable example is the cuckoo clock, a symbol of the region's craftsmanship. The House of 1000 Clocks, located at Hauptstraße 79-81, 78098 Triberg, offers a wide range of authentic, handmade cuckoo clocks. Prices range from $50 for small, simple designs to over $1000 for intricate, large pieces.

When shopping for souvenirs, look for items that are made locally and sustainably. For example, the Black Forest's famous wooden toys and carvings are often crafted from sustainably harvested wood. Visit local markets, such as the Freiburg Minster Market, held daily except Sundays at Münsterplatz, 79098 Freiburg. Here, you can find a variety of handmade goods, from pottery to textiles, ensuring your money supports local artisans.

Always ask about the origin of the products you buy. Many shops are happy to provide information about the materials used and the artisans who made them. This ensures that your purchases are not only unique but also contribute to the local economy in a sustainable manner.

2. Local Tours and Guides

Exploring the Black Forest with a local guide can enhance your experience and provide valuable insights into the region's culture and history. Opting for local tours also supports the community. Black Forest Tours, located at Basler Straße 8, 79100 Freiburg, offers a variety of eco-friendly tours, from hiking excursions to cultural tours of quaint villages. Prices for guided hikes start at $50 per person for a half-day tour.

For a more immersive experience, consider booking a tour with the Naturpark Südschwarzwald guides. These certified guides offer educational tours focusing on the region's natural and cultural heritage. Tours are tailored to small groups to minimize environmental impact and usually cost around $40 per person for a half-day trip.

Booking a local guide not only enriches your travel experience but also ensures that your money benefits the local community directly. Guides can share lesser-known spots and provide context that you might miss on your own, making your visit more meaningful.

9.3 Reducing Your Carbon Footprint

1. Public Transport

The Black Forest boasts an efficient and eco-friendly public transportation network, making it easy to reduce your carbon footprint while exploring the region. Trains and buses are the most sustainable modes of transport. The Konus Card, available to guests staying in participating accommodations, offers free travel on regional trains and buses throughout the Black Forest. This card can save you a significant amount on transportation costs and encourage the use of public transport over private cars.

One of the most scenic train routes is the Black Forest Railway, running from Offenburg to Konstanz. The journey offers breathtaking views of the region's landscapes and costs around $30 for a one-way ticket. Buses also connect major towns and attractions, providing a convenient and green way to travel.

To get the most out of public transport, plan your routes in advance and take advantage of day passes or travel cards. These options often provide unlimited travel within a specific area and can be more economical than purchasing individual tickets.

2. Cycling and Walking

Cycling and walking are not only sustainable ways to explore the Black Forest but also provide a more intimate experience of its natural beauty. The region is crisscrossed with well-maintained cycling paths and walking trails, suitable for all fitness levels. The Schwarzwald-Panorama-Radweg, a 280-mile cycling route, offers spectacular views and passes through charming villages and dense forests.

Bike rentals are widely available, with prices ranging from $20 to $40 per day. For instance, Freiburg's Radstation, located at Wentzingerstraße 15, 79106 Freiburg, offers a variety of bicycles, including e-bikes for those who need a little extra help on hilly terrain.

Walking is another fantastic way to reduce your carbon footprint while enjoying the scenery. The Black Forest offers numerous hiking trails, from short, easy walks to challenging multi-day hikes. One popular route is the Feldbergsteig, a 7.5-mile loop trail around the Feldberg, the highest peak in the Black Forest. The trail offers stunning views and costs nothing to explore, making it a budget-friendly and eco-friendly activity.

To make the most of cycling and walking, always carry a reusable water bottle and snacks to avoid unnecessary waste. Wear comfortable shoes and weather-appropriate clothing, and respect the natural environment by staying on marked trails and not disturbing wildlife.

By incorporating these sustainable practices into your travel plans, you can enjoy the Black Forest's beauty while minimizing your environmental impact and supporting local communities.

CHAPTER TEN
PRACTICAL INFORMATION
10.1 Language and Communication
Basic Phrases

- Greetings and General Phrases
- Hallo - Hello
- Guten Morgen - Good morning
- Guten Tag - Good day
- Guten Abend - Good evening
- Gute Nacht - Good night
- Tschüss - Bye
- Auf Wiedersehen - Goodbye
- Wie geht es Ihnen? - How are you? (formal)
- Wie geht's? - How are you? (informal)
- Mir geht es gut, danke - I am good, thank you
- Bitte - Please
- Danke - Thank you
- Entschuldigung - Excuse me / Sorry
- Ja - Yes
- Nein - No

Essential Questions

- Sprechen Sie Englisch? - Do you speak English?
- Wie viel kostet das? - How much does this cost?
- Wo ist...? - Where is...?
- Wie komme ich zu...? - How do I get to...?
- Wann öffnet/schließt...? - When does ... open/close?
- Können Sie mir helfen? - Can you help me?
- Was empfehlen Sie? - What do you recommend?

At the Restaurant

- Ich hätte gern... - I would like...
- Die Speisekarte, bitte - The menu, please
- Ein Glas Wasser, bitte - A glass of water, please
- Das Essen war sehr gut - The food was very good
- Könnte ich bitte die Rechnung haben? - Could I have the bill, please?
- Trinkgeld - Tip
- Frühstück - Breakfast
- Mittagessen - Lunch
- Abendessen - Dinner
- Vegetarisch - Vegetarian
- Ich bin allergisch gegen... - I am allergic to...

At the Hotel

- Ich habe eine Reservierung - I have a reservation
- Könnte ich ein Zimmer für eine Nacht haben? - Could I have a room for one night?
- Gibt es WLAN? - Is there Wi-Fi?
- Wie ist das Passwort für das WLAN? - What is the Wi-Fi password?
- Könnte ich bitte einen Weckruf haben? - Could I have a wake-up call, please?
- Wo ist der Frühstücksraum? - Where is the breakfast room?

Shopping

- Kann ich mit Karte bezahlen? - Can I pay with a card?
- Haben Sie das in einer anderen Größe? - Do you have this in another size?
- Haben Sie das in einer anderen Farbe? - Do you have this in another color?

- Kann ich eine Quittung bekommen? - Can I get a receipt?
- Ich schaue nur, danke - I am just looking, thank you

Transportation

- Wo ist die nächste Bushaltestelle? - Where is the nearest bus stop?
- Ein Ticket nach..., bitte - A ticket to..., please
- Wann fährt der nächste Zug nach...? - When does the next train to... leave?
- Wie lange dauert die Fahrt nach...? - How long does the trip to... take?
- Müssen wir umsteigen? - Do we need to change trains/buses?
- Könnte ich ein Taxi rufen? - Could I call a taxi?

Emergencies

- Hilfe! - Help!
- Rufen Sie die Polizei! - Call the police!
- Ich brauche einen Arzt - I need a doctor
- Wo ist das nächste Krankenhaus? - Where is the nearest hospital?
- Ich habe mich verlaufen - I am lost
- Gibt es eine Apotheke in der Nähe? - Is there a pharmacy nearby?

Directions

- Rechts - Right
- Links - Left
- Geradeaus - Straight ahead
- Nach oben - Up
- Nach unten - Down

- In der Nähe - Nearby
- Weit - Far
- In der Nähe von... - Near...

Numbers

- Eins - One
- Zwei - Two
- Drei - Three
- Vier - Four
- Fünf - Five
- Sechs - Six
- Sieben - Seven
- Acht - Eight
- Neun - Nine
- Zehn - Ten
- Zwanzig - Twenty
- Dreißig - Thirty
- Vierzig - Forty
- Fünfzig - Fifty
- Sechzig - Sixty
- Siebzig - Seventy
- Achtzig - Eighty
- Neunzig - Ninety
- Hundert - One hundred

These phrases and vocabulary will help you navigate your visit to the Black Forest with more confidence and ease. Remember, even a small effort to speak the local language can greatly enhance your travel experience.

English Speakers

While German is the primary language spoken in the Black Forest, you will find that English is commonly spoken in larger towns and cities, particularly in tourist hotspots like Freiburg, Baden-Baden, and Triberg. The hospitality industry staff, such as hotel employees, restaurant servers, and tour guides, often speak English to cater to international visitors. Tourist information centers in these areas usually have English-speaking staff who can assist with maps, brochures, and travel advice.

Example in Use: At the Freiburg Tourist Information Center located at Rathausplatz 2-4, 79098 Freiburg, you can ask for an English-language map of the city. The staff can also provide recommendations on local attractions and dining options in fluent English.

However, in smaller villages and rural parts of the Black Forest, English may not be as widely spoken. Here, a few basic German phrases and a friendly attitude can go a long way. Consider downloading a translation app on your smartphone or carrying a small phrasebook to bridge any language gaps. These tools can help you read menus, understand signs, and communicate with locals who might not speak English.

Example in Use: When exploring the charming village of Sasbachwalden, known for its beautiful vineyards and half-timbered houses, you might visit a local winery. While the winemaker might speak limited English, using phrases like "Können wir den Wein probieren?" (Can we taste the wine?) can enhance your experience and show respect for the local culture.

Tips for Learning and Using Basic Phrases

- Practice Before You Go: Familiarize yourself with basic phrases before your trip. There are many

language learning apps, such as Duolingo or Babbel, that can help you practice.
- Listen and Imitate: Pay attention to how locals pronounce words and try to imitate their accent and intonation.
- Be Patient and Polite: If you don't understand something, don't hesitate to ask the speaker to repeat or speak slowly. Most people will appreciate your effort and be happy to help.
- Use Technology: Translation apps like Google Translate can be very handy for quick translations. Some apps even offer real-time translation through your phone's camera for menus and signs.

Example in Use: If you're at a local bakery and want to buy some traditional Black Forest cake, you could say, "Ich hätte gern ein Stück Schwarzwälder Kirschtorte, bitte" (I would like a piece of Black Forest cake, please). If you don't understand the response, you can politely ask, "Können Sie das wiederholen?" (Can you repeat that?).

10.2 Currency and Banking
Exchange Rates

Germany uses the Euro (€). As of mid-2024, the exchange rate is approximately 1 USD = 0.85 EUR, but this can fluctuate. It's advisable to check the current rate before your trip. You can exchange money at banks, currency exchange offices, and some hotels. Major airports and train stations also offer currency exchange services, though they may charge higher fees.

ATMs and Credit Cards

ATMs are widely available throughout the Black Forest. Using your debit or credit card at ATMs is often the most convenient way to get Euros, and it usually offers a better exchange rate than currency exchange offices. Look for ATMs marked with symbols of international networks like Visa, MasterCard, and Cirrus.

Most restaurants, hotels, and shops accept major credit cards, but it's wise to carry some cash for smaller establishments, especially in rural areas. Note that some places might have a minimum amount for card payments.

10.3 Internet and Connectivity
1. Wi-Fi Availability

Wi-Fi is readily available in the Black Forest, particularly in hotels, cafes, and restaurants. Many towns offer free public Wi-Fi in central areas, such as main squares and tourist information centers. Freiburg, for example, provides free Wi-Fi through the "Freiburg WiFi" network in various parts of the city, including the Old Town and main shopping streets.

2. SIM Cards and Mobile Data

If you need mobile data, purchasing a local SIM card is a cost-effective solution. You can buy SIM cards from major providers like Deutsche Telekom, Vodafone, and O2 at their stores or at kiosks and electronics shops. Plans typically range from €10 to €30, depending on the amount of data and duration.

To get the most out of your mobile data:

- Choose a plan that matches your data needs. A €20 plan usually includes around 5-10GB of data, sufficient for a week of moderate use.
- Ensure your phone is unlocked and compatible with European networks.

- Consider using messaging apps like WhatsApp, which are popular in Germany, for staying in touch.

10.4 Safety and Security
1. Staying Safe

The Black Forest is generally very safe for travelers, but it's always wise to take standard precautions:

- Keep an eye on your belongings, especially in crowded areas.
- Avoid walking alone at night in unfamiliar places.
- Use hotel safes for valuables.
- Be cautious of your surroundings when using ATMs.

2. Emergency Contacts

In case of an emergency, dial 112 for police, fire, or medical assistance. This is the universal emergency number in Germany and throughout the European Union.

Here are some important contacts to keep handy:

- Police: 112
- Ambulance: 112
- Fire Brigade: 112

Tourist Information Centers: These can provide assistance in non-emergency situations and help with lost items or travel issues.

10.5 Accessibility
1. For Disabled Travelers

The Black Forest is becoming increasingly accessible for travelers with disabilities, but it's essential to plan ahead.

Major cities like Freiburg and Baden-Baden have good accessibility features, including:

- Public Transportation: Many buses and trams are wheelchair accessible, with ramps and designated spaces.
- Accommodations: Hotels often have rooms equipped for disabled guests. It's best to confirm specific needs when booking.
- Attractions: Many tourist sites, such as the Freiburg Minster and the Baden-Baden thermal baths, have made efforts to improve accessibility.

2. Resources and Support

Several organizations and resources can assist disabled travelers:

- Accessible Travel Germany: Provides information and resources for traveling in Germany with a disability.
- Tourist Information Centers: Offer guidance on accessible attractions and accommodations.
- Mobility Equipment Rental: Some companies rent wheelchairs, mobility scooters, and other equipment. For example, "Medical Travel Service" in Freiburg provides a range of rental options.

Travelers should communicate their needs in advance to ensure a smooth and enjoyable trip. With proper planning, the Black Forest can be a rewarding destination for all visitors.

CHAPTER ELEVEN
TRAVEL ITINERARIES

11.1 One-Week Highlights Tour

Day 1: Arrival in Freiburg im Breisgau

Morning: Arrive in Freiburg im Breisgau, a charming city known for its medieval architecture and vibrant cultural scene. Check into your accommodation at the Colombi Hotel, a five-star luxury hotel located at Rotteckring 16, 79098 Freiburg. The hotel offers top-notch amenities including a spa, gourmet dining, and elegant rooms. Average nightly rates are around $300.

Afternoon: Explore the Freiburg Minster, an impressive Gothic cathedral dating back to the 13th century. Climb the 116-meter tower for a panoramic view of the city. Entry to the tower is $5. Afterward, stroll through the Münsterplatz market (open daily except Sundays), where you can sample local delicacies like Black Forest ham and cherry schnapps.

Evening: Dine at Hausbrauerei Feierling, a local brewery and restaurant located at Gerberau 46. Enjoy traditional German dishes and craft beers. A meal here costs around $25 per person.

Day 2: Discover Baden-Baden

Morning: Travel to Baden-Baden, a picturesque spa town about an hour's drive from Freiburg. Start your day at the Caracalla Spa (Römerplatz 1), known for its thermal baths and wellness treatments. The spa opens at 8 a.m., and a 3-hour pass costs $25. Enjoy the indoor and outdoor pools, steam baths, and saunas.

Afternoon: Visit the Museum Frieder Burda (Lichtentaler Allee 8b), which showcases contemporary art. Admission is $15. Take a leisurely walk along Lichtentaler Allee, a beautiful park and arboretum.

Evening: Try your luck at the elegant Kurhaus Casino (Kaiserallee 1), open from 2 p.m. to 2 a.m. Entry costs $7.50. Dine at Rizzi WineBistro & Restaurant (Augustaplatz 1), known for its sophisticated cuisine and extensive wine list. Expect to spend around $50 per person.

Day 3: Triberg and Its Waterfalls

Morning: Head to Triberg, famous for its waterfalls and cuckoo clocks. The Triberg Waterfalls (open daily from 9 a.m. to 5 p.m.) are among the highest in Germany. The entry fee is $5. Hike the well-marked trails for spectacular views.

Afternoon: Visit the Black Forest Museum (Wallfahrtstraße 4), which offers insights into regional traditions and crafts. Admission is $8. Don't miss the House of 1000 Clocks (Hauptstraße 82), where you can purchase an authentic cuckoo clock. Prices vary, but expect to spend at least $50.

Evening: Enjoy dinner at Parkhotel Wehrle (Gartenstraße 24), offering local specialties in an elegant setting. Dinner for two costs around $70.

Day 4: Titisee and Feldberg

Morning: Drive to Titisee, a beautiful lake in the heart of the Black Forest. Rent a paddleboat from Bootsvermietung Tretboote (Seestraße 33), open from 10 a.m. to 6 p.m. Boat rental costs $15 per hour. Enjoy the serene waters and surrounding scenery.

Afternoon: Head to Feldberg, the highest peak in the Black Forest. Take the Feldbergbahn cable car (open from 9 a.m. to 5 p.m.) to the summit. A round-trip ticket costs $12. Enjoy hiking or simply soak in the panoramic views.

Evening: Return to Titisee and dine at Seehotel Wiesler (Seestraße 25), which offers lake views and regional dishes. A meal here costs about $30 per person.

Day 5: Adventure in Baiersbronn

Morning: Travel to Baiersbronn, renowned for its hiking trails and gourmet dining. Start with a hike on the Sankenbach Waterfall Trail, a moderate 6-kilometer route offering beautiful forest views and cascading waterfalls.

Afternoon: Visit the Hauff's Fairy Tale Museum (Murgtalstraße 1), open from 11 a.m. to 5 p.m. Admission is $6. Learn about local folklore and fairy tales in this charming museum.

Evening: Dine at the three-Michelin-starred Schwarzwaldstube (Tonbachstraße 237), known for its exquisite cuisine. Expect to spend around $200 per person for a tasting menu.

Day 6: Explore Offenburg and Surroundings

Morning: Drive to Offenburg, a town known for its wine and half-timbered houses. Visit the Ortenau Wine Museum (Weinbrennerstraße 6), open from 10 a.m. to 5 p.m. Admission is $7. Learn about the region's wine-making traditions.

Afternoon: Take a scenic drive along the Badische Weinstraße (Baden Wine Route), stopping at local vineyards for wine tastings. Many vineyards offer tastings for $10-$15 per person.

Evening: Enjoy dinner at Brandeck Vineyard (Brandeckstraße 16), which offers excellent local cuisine and wines. A meal costs around $40 per person.

Day 7: Departure

Morning: Spend your final morning in Freiburg, visiting any sights you may have missed. Consider a relaxing walk through the Stadtgarten (City Garden) or a final visit to the Freiburg Minster.

Afternoon: Depart for your next destination or head back home, taking with you unforgettable memories of the Black Forest.

11.2 Family-Friendly Adventure
Day 1: Arrival in Freiburg im Breisgau

Morning: Arrive in Freiburg im Breisgau and check into your family-friendly hotel. The Novotel Freiburg am Konzerthaus (Konrad-Adenauer-Platz 2), offers family rooms and amenities such as a play area and pool. Rates start at $150 per night.

Afternoon: Visit the Freiburg Minster and take a guided tour tailored for children. These tours often include interactive elements and storytelling to engage young minds. Entry and the tour together cost around $10 per person.

Evening: Enjoy a family dinner at Kartoffelhaus (Basler Straße 10), where kids can enjoy dishes made from various types of potatoes while adults can try regional specialties. Expect to spend about $60 for a family of four.

Day 2: Europapark Adventure

Morning: Spend the day at Europapark (Europa-Park-Straße 2, Rust), Germany's largest theme park, located about an hour from Freiburg. The park opens at 9 a.m., and tickets are $55 for adults and $47 for children.

Afternoon: Explore the different themed areas of the park, each representing a European country. Enjoy roller coasters, water rides, and live shows. There are plenty of dining options within the park, with meals averaging $15 per person.

Evening: Return to Freiburg for a restful night. Consider a light dinner at your hotel or a nearby café.

Day 3: Titisee Lake and Badeparadies Schwarzwald

Morning: Head to Titisee, a picturesque lake ideal for family activities. Rent a pedal boat or take a leisurely walk around the lake. Boat rentals cost $15 per hour.

Afternoon: Visit Badeparadies Schwarzwald (Am Badeparadies 1, Titisee-Neustadt), an indoor water park with slides, pools, and a tropical area for relaxation. Entry fees are $30 for adults and $20 for children for a 3-hour pass. The park opens at 10 a.m.

Evening: Have dinner at Seehotel Wiesler's family-friendly restaurant, which offers kid-friendly menus and stunning lake views. Expect to spend about $70 for a family of four.

Day 4: Black Forest Open-Air Museum

Morning: Drive to the Black Forest Open-Air Museum (Vogtsbauernhof, Gutach), where you can explore historic farmhouses and learn about traditional Black Forest life. The museum opens at 10 a.m., and admission is $12 for adults and $6 for children.

Afternoon: Participate in hands-on workshops like bread baking or pottery, designed to engage children and teach them about local crafts. Workshop fees are around $10 per person.

Evening: Return to Freiburg and dine at Trattoria im Primo-Markt (Lehener Straße 14), a family-friendly Italian restaurant. Meals cost around $50 for a family of four.

Day 5: Exploring Triberg

Morning: Visit Triberg and start with the Triberg Waterfalls, the highest in Germany. Entry is $5. Kids will love the easy trails and the chance to feed the ducks and fish in the streams.

Afternoon: Explore the Black Forest Museum and House of 1000 Clocks. These attractions offer interactive exhibits and demonstrations of cuckoo clock making. Combined entry costs around $10 per person.

Evening: Enjoy dinner at Parkhotel Wehrle, which offers a children's menu and regional dishes. Dinner for a family costs about $70.

Day 6: Adventure in Baiersbronn

Morning: Travel to Baiersbronn for a day of outdoor fun. Start with a family-friendly hike on the Sankenbach Waterfall Trail. It's a moderate 6-kilometer route that's suitable for kids.

Afternoon: Visit the Hauff's Fairy Tale Museum, which features interactive displays and fairy tale characters. Admission is $6. The museum opens at 11 a.m.

Evening: Dine at a local restaurant such as Sattelei (Schiffwiesenstraße 31), which offers hearty German cuisine and a cozy atmosphere. Expect to spend around $60 for a family meal.

Day 7: Departure

Morning: Spend your final morning in Freiburg, perhaps visiting the local farmer's market for some last-minute souvenirs or enjoying a relaxing walk in the Stadtgarten.

Afternoon: Check out of your hotel and prepare for your journey home, reflecting on the wonderful family memories made in the Black Forest.

11.3 Solo Traveler's Journey
Day 1: Arrival in Freiburg im Breisgau

Morning: Arrive in Freiburg and check into a centrally located hostel like Black Forest Hostel (Kartäuserstraße 33). Dormitory beds cost around $25 per night.

Afternoon: Explore the Old Town, starting with the Freiburg Minster. Join a guided walking tour to learn about the city's history and architecture. Tours typically cost $15.

Evening: Dine at Martin's Bräu (Kaiser-Joseph-Straße 237), a local brewery offering a lively atmosphere and affordable meals around $20.

Day 2: Hiking the Schauinsland

Morning: Take a tram to the base of Schauinsland mountain and ride the cable car to the summit. A round-trip ticket costs $12. Hike one of the many trails, enjoying panoramic views and the fresh mountain air.

Afternoon: Visit the Schniederlihof Museum (Museumsweg 1), a preserved 18th-century farmstead, for a glimpse into rural life. Entry is $6. The museum opens at 11 a.m.

Evening: Return to Freiburg and grab a quick bite at Euphrat (Bertoldstraße 45), a popular spot for kebabs and falafel. Meals cost around $10.

Day 3: Day Trip to Heidelberg

Morning: Take a train to Heidelberg, a charming city known for its historic castle and university. The journey takes about 2 hours and costs $20 each way.

Afternoon: Explore Heidelberg Castle (Schlosshof 1), with its stunning views over the Neckar River. Admission is $10. Visit the University Museum and stroll through the Old Town.

Evening: Return to Freiburg and dine at Kartoffelhaus. Meals cost about $20.

Day 4: Exploring Baden-Baden

Morning: Travel to Baden-Baden, about an hour from Freiburg. Start your day at the Caracalla Spa, with a 3-hour pass costing $25. Relax in the thermal baths and saunas.

Afternoon: Visit the Museum Frieder Burda, which showcases contemporary art. Admission is $15. Walk along Lichtentaler Allee, enjoying the beautiful gardens and sculptures.

Evening: Have dinner at Rizzi WineBistro & Restaurant, spending around $40. Return to Freiburg for the night.

Day 5: Titisee and Feldberg

Morning: Visit Titisee, where you can rent a paddleboat for $15 per hour or take a walk around the lake.

Afternoon: Head to Feldberg and take the cable car to the summit. A round-trip ticket costs $12. Hike or simply enjoy the views.

Evening: Return to Freiburg and have a casual dinner at Euphrat. Meals cost around $10.

Day 6: Cultural Immersion in Offenburg

Morning: Travel to Offenburg and visit the Ortenau Wine Museum. Admission is $7. Learn about the region's wine-making traditions.

Afternoon: Take a scenic drive along the Badische Weinstraße, stopping at vineyards for wine tastings. Tastings cost $10-$15 per person.

Evening: Have dinner at Brandeck Vineyard, enjoying local cuisine and wines. Meals cost around $40. Return to Freiburg for the night.

Day 7: Departure

Morning: Spend your final morning in Freiburg, perhaps visiting any sights you may have missed or enjoying a relaxing walk in the Stadtgarten.

Afternoon: Check out of your hostel and prepare for your journey home, cherishing the solo adventures experienced in the Black Forest.

11.4 Romantic Getaways
Day 1: Arrival in Freiburg im Breisgau

Morning: Arrive in Freiburg and check into the Colombi Hotel, known for its luxurious amenities and romantic ambiance. Average nightly rates are around $300.

Afternoon: Visit the Freiburg Minster and enjoy a climb to the tower for breathtaking views. The entry fee is $5. Stroll through the Münsterplatz market, sampling local delicacies.

Evening: Have a romantic dinner at Restaurant Dattler (Schlossbergring 3), offering stunning views and exquisite cuisine. Expect to spend around $100 for a romantic dinner for two.

Day 2: Relaxing in Baden-Baden

Morning: Travel to Baden-Baden and start your day at the Caracalla Spa. A 3-hour pass costs $25. Enjoy the thermal baths, saunas, and wellness treatments.

Afternoon: Visit the Museum Frieder Burda and take a leisurely walk along Lichtentaler Allee. Admission to the museum is $15.

Evening: Dine at Le Jardin de France (Lichtentaler Straße 13), a Michelin-starred restaurant offering an intimate dining experience. Expect to spend around $200 for a meal for two.

Day 3: Exploring Triberg

Morning: Head to Triberg and start with the Triberg Waterfalls, one of the highest in Germany. The entry fee is $5. Enjoy a romantic hike along the trails.

Afternoon: Visit the Black Forest Museum and House of 1000 Clocks. Combined entry costs around $10 per person.

Evening: Enjoy a romantic dinner at Parkhotel Wehrle, known for its charming setting and regional dishes. Dinner for two costs about $70.

Day 4: Titisee and Feldberg

Morning: Visit Titisee and rent a paddleboat for a romantic ride on the lake. Boat rentals cost $15 per hour.

Afternoon: Head to Feldberg and take the cable car to the summit. A round-trip ticket costs $12. Enjoy hiking or simply soak in the panoramic views.

Evening: Return to Titisee and dine at Seehotel Wiesler, offering lake views and regional dishes. A meal here costs about $60 for two.

Day 5: Adventure in Baiersbronn

Morning: Travel to Baiersbronn and start with a hike on the Sankenbach Waterfall Trail. It's a moderate 6-kilometer route offering beautiful forest views.

Afternoon: Visit the Hauff's Fairy Tale Museum, which features interactive displays and fairy tale characters. Admission is $6.

Evening: Dine at the three-Michelin-starred Schwarzwaldstube, known for its exquisite cuisine. Expect to spend around $400 for a tasting menu for two.

Day 6: Wine Tasting in Offenburg

Morning: Drive to Offenburg and visit the Ortenau Wine Museum. Admission is $7. Learn about the region's wine-making traditions.

Afternoon: Take a scenic drive along the Badische Weinstraße, stopping at vineyards for wine tastings. Many vineyards offer tastings for $10-$15 per person.

Evening: Enjoy a romantic dinner at Brandeck Vineyard, which offers excellent local cuisine and wines. A meal costs around $80 for two.

Day 7: Departure

Morning: Spend your final morning in Freiburg, perhaps visiting any sights you may have missed or enjoying a relaxing walk in the Stadtgarten.

Afternoon: Check out of your hotel and prepare for your journey home, taking with you unforgettable memories of your romantic getaway in the Black Forest.

11.5 Off-the-Beaten-Path Excursions
Day 1: Arrival in Freiburg im Breisgau

Morning: Arrive in Freiburg and check into a centrally located boutique hotel like Hotel Oberkirch (Münsterplatz 22). Rooms here cost around $120 per night.

Afternoon: Explore the lesser-known parts of Freiburg, such as the Augustiner Museum, which houses a collection of medieval art and artifacts. Admission is $8. The museum opens at 10 a.m.

Evening: Dine at Wolfshöhle (Herrenstraße 5), a hidden gem offering gourmet dishes in an intimate setting. Meals cost around $60 per person.

Day 2: Hidden Villages and Scenic Drives

Morning: Drive to the quaint village of St. Peter, known for its Baroque abbey (Klosterhof 2). The abbey is open to visitors from 10 a.m. to 6 p.m. and entry is free. Stroll through the village and enjoy the serene atmosphere.

Afternoon: Continue to the village of St. Märgen, famous for its monastery (Erwin-Sick-Straße 13). Visit the monastery and enjoy the surrounding landscapes.

Evening: Return to Freiburg and have dinner at Gasthaus Zum Kranz (Schwarzwaldstraße 1), known for its local cuisine. Expect to spend around $50 for a meal.

Day 3: Gengenbach and Surroundings

Morning: Travel to Gengenbach, a small town with beautifully preserved half-timbered houses. Explore the town's historic center and visit the Gengenbach Town Hall (Hauptstraße 1), known for its unique Advent calendar.

Afternoon: Take a hike in the surrounding vineyards, enjoying the scenic views and peaceful trails.

Evening: Dine at Pfeffermühle (Reichenbacher Hauptstraße 18), offering regional dishes in a cozy setting. Meals cost around $40 per person. Return to Freiburg for the night.

Day 4: Calw and the Hermann Hesse Museum

Morning: Drive to Calw, the birthplace of Hermann Hesse. Visit the Hermann Hesse Museum (Marktplatz 30), which opens at 11 a.m. and costs $6. The museum offers insights into the life and works of the Nobel Prize-winning author.

Afternoon: Explore the charming town of Calw, with its narrow streets and historic buildings. Enjoy a coffee at a local café and soak in the town's literary atmosphere.

Evening: Return to Freiburg and dine at a local restaurant such as Wolfshöhle. Meals cost around $60 per person.

Day 5: Nature and Tranquility in Todtnau

Morning: Head to Todtnau, known for its stunning waterfalls (Hanglochweg 76). The falls are open to visitors all day and entry is free. Hike the trails around the falls for a refreshing experience.

Afternoon: Visit the Hasenhorn Coaster (Schützenstraße 1), a mountain coaster that offers thrilling rides through the forest. Tickets cost $10. The coaster opens at 10 a.m.

Evening: Return to Freiburg and have dinner at Wolfshöhle. Meals cost around $60 per person.

Day 6: History and Culture in Schiltach

Morning: Drive to Schiltach, a historic town with well-preserved timber-framed houses. Visit the Museum am Markt (Marktplatz 1), which showcases local history and culture. Admission is $5.

Afternoon: Explore the town's scenic streets and enjoy a peaceful walk along the Kinzig River.

Evening: Dine at Zur alten Brücke (Hauptstraße 19), offering traditional dishes in a charming setting. Meals cost around $40 per person. Return to Freiburg for the night.

Day 7: Departure

Morning: Spend your final morning in Freiburg, visiting any sights you may have missed or enjoying a relaxing walk in the Stadtgarten.

Afternoon: Check out of your hotel and prepare for your journey home, reflecting on the unique and lesser-known experiences of the Black Forest.

11.6 Outdoor Adventures

Day 1: Arrival in Freiburg im Breisgau

Morning: Arrive in Freiburg and check into a centrally located hostel like Black Forest Hostel (Kartäuserstraße 33). Dormitory beds cost around $25 per night.

Afternoon: Explore the Old Town, starting with the Freiburg Minster. Join a guided walking tour to learn about the city's history and architecture. Tours typically cost $15.

Evening: Dine at Martin's Bräu (Kaiser-Joseph-Straße 237), a local brewery offering a lively atmosphere and affordable meals around $20.

Day 2: Hiking the Schauinsland

Morning: Take a tram to the base of Schauinsland mountain and ride the cable car to the summit. A round-trip ticket costs $12. Hike one of the many trails, enjoying panoramic views and the fresh mountain air.

Afternoon: Visit the Schniederlihof Museum (Museumsweg 1), a preserved 18th-century farmstead, for a glimpse into rural life. Entry is $6. The museum opens at 11 a.m.

Evening: Return to Freiburg and grab a quick bite at Euphrat (Bertoldstraße 45), a popular spot for kebabs and falafel. Meals cost around $10.

Day 3: Mountain Biking in Todtnau

Morning: Head to Todtnau, a paradise for mountain biking enthusiasts. Rent a mountain bike from Todtnau Bikepark (Ennerbachstraße 60), with full-day rentals costing $40.

Afternoon: Explore the various trails, ranging from beginner to advanced levels. The Todtnau Bikepark offers stunning views and thrilling rides. A day pass for the park costs $20.

Evening: Return to Freiburg and have dinner at Euphrat. Meals cost around $10.

Day 4: Water Sports at Lake Titisee

Morning: Visit Titisee, where you can rent a paddleboard or kayak from Bootsvermietung Tretboote (Seestraße 33). Rentals cost $20 per hour.

Afternoon: Enjoy the serene waters of Lake Titisee and the beautiful surrounding scenery.

Evening: Dine at Seehotel Wiesler, offering lake views and regional dishes. A meal here costs about $30 per person.

Day 5: Paragliding in Badenweiler

Morning: Drive to Badenweiler and experience the thrill of paragliding. Tandem flights with Paragliding Black Forest (Römerstraße 5) cost $150 and offer breathtaking views of the region.

Afternoon: Relax in the Cassiopeia Thermal Baths (Ernst-Eisenlohr-Straße 1), which opens at 9 a.m. and costs $25 for a 3-hour pass.

Evening: Return to Freiburg and dine at Martin's Bräu. Meals cost around $20.

Day 6: Adventure in Baiersbronn

Morning: Travel to Baiersbronn and start with a hike on the Sankenbach Waterfall Trail. It's a moderate 6-kilometer route offering beautiful forest views.

Afternoon: Visit the Hauff's Fairy Tale Museum, which features interactive displays and fairy tale characters. Admission is $6.

Evening: Dine at a local restaurant such as Sattelei (Schiffwiesenstraße 31), which offers hearty German cuisine and a cozy atmosphere. Expect to spend around $60 for a family meal.

Day 7: Departure

Morning: Spend your final morning in Freiburg, visiting any sights you may have missed or enjoying a relaxing walk in the Stadtgarten.

Afternoon: Check out of your hotel and prepare for your journey home, reflecting on the unique and lesser-known experiences of the Black Forest.

APPENDIX
USEFUL RESOURCES
A. Websites and Apps
Travel Planning Tools

Planning your trip to the Black Forest can be both exciting and overwhelming. Fortunately, numerous websites and apps are designed to help streamline your travel preparations, ensuring you get the most out of your visit.

1. Deutsche Bahn (DB)

Website: bahn.com

The Deutsche Bahn website is a crucial tool for anyone planning to travel by train within Germany. It offers schedules, ticket prices, and the ability to book tickets online. The website is user-friendly and available in multiple languages, including English. The DB Navigator app complements the website, providing real-time updates on train schedules and platform information, which is particularly useful for navigating the extensive rail network in the Black Forest.

2. TripAdvisor

Website: tripadvisor.com

TripAdvisor is a well-known platform for traveler reviews and recommendations. It's an excellent resource for finding the best hotels, restaurants, and attractions in the Black Forest. The site features user-generated content, offering diverse opinions and tips from fellow travelers. The mobile app allows you to read reviews and view ratings on the go, helping you make informed decisions during your trip.

3. Booking.com

Website: booking.com

For booking accommodations, Booking.com is one of the most reliable platforms. It offers a wide range of options, from luxury hotels to budget-friendly guesthouses. The site includes user reviews, detailed descriptions, and photos, ensuring you can find the perfect place to stay. Booking.com often provides special deals and discounts, making it a great tool for budget-conscious travelers.

Local Information

1. Schwarzwald App

Available on: iOS and Android

The Schwarzwald app is a comprehensive guide to the Black Forest, available for both iOS and Android devices. It features interactive maps, suggested itineraries, and detailed information on attractions, restaurants, and accommodations. The app also includes GPS-based navigation, making it easy to explore the region's trails and scenic routes without getting lost. Additionally, it provides up-to-date weather forecasts and information on local events.

2. Komoot

Available on: iOS and Android

Komoot is a must-have app for outdoor enthusiasts visiting the Black Forest. It's designed specifically for planning and navigating outdoor activities such as hiking, cycling, and mountain biking. The app allows you to create custom routes based on your preferences and skill level, and it provides turn-by-turn navigation to keep you on track. Komoot's detailed maps include elevation profiles, helping you prepare for the terrain you'll encounter.

3. Black Forest Discovery App

Available on: iOS and Android

The Black Forest Discovery app offers an immersive way to learn about the region's history, culture, and natural beauty. It includes audio guides, interactive maps, and augmented reality features that bring local attractions to life. The app is particularly useful for families, as it offers engaging content for children, making sightseeing more fun and educational.

B. Contact Information
Tourist Offices

1. Freiburg Tourist Information

- Address: Rathausplatz 2-4, 79098 Freiburg im Breisgau
- Website: visit.freiburg.de

The Freiburg Tourist Information office is located in the heart of the city, providing visitors with maps, brochures, and personalized advice on local attractions and events. The friendly staff can assist with booking accommodations, guided tours, and transportation.

2. Baden-Baden Tourism

- Address: Solmsstraße 1, 76530 Baden-Baden
- Website: baden-baden.com

Baden-Baden's tourist office offers a wealth of information on the town's famous spas, cultural sites, and luxury experiences. They can help with recommendations for dining, shopping, and outdoor activities, ensuring you make the most of your visit.

3. Black Forest Tourism Board

- Address: Heinrich-von-Stephan-Straße 8b, 79100 Freiburg im Breisgau

The Black Forest Tourism Board's office is a central resource for planning your trip. They provide detailed information on all aspects of the region, from hiking trails to culinary experiences. Their website is also a valuable tool, offering downloadable maps and travel guides.

Local Authorities

1. Police Department (Polizei)

In case of emergency, dial 110 for the police.

For non-emergency situations, contact the local police department:

- Address: Bertoldstraße 43, 79098 Freiburg im Breisgau

The local police department in Freiburg can assist with any security or safety concerns. They are available 24/7 and can provide help in English.

2. Medical Services

For medical emergencies, dial 112 for an ambulance.

For non-emergency medical assistance:

- Address: Universitätsklinikum Freiburg, Hugstetter Str. 55, 79106 Freiburg im Breisgau
- Website: uniklinik-freiburg.de

The University Medical Center Freiburg is one of the top hospitals in the region, offering comprehensive medical services. They have a dedicated team of English-speaking staff to assist international patients.

3. Consulates

If you require consular assistance, several consulates are located in Stuttgart, a short distance from the Black Forest:

1. United States Consulate General

- Address: Königinstraße 30, 70173 Stuttgart

2. United Kingdom Consulate General

- Address: Richard-Wagner-Straße 1, 70184 Stuttgart

These consulates can assist with passport issues, legal matters, and emergency situations. Always carry a copy of your passport and contact information for your nearest consulate.

By utilizing these resources, you can ensure a smooth and enjoyable trip to the Black Forest. From planning your itinerary with helpful websites and apps to knowing where to turn for assistance, you'll be well-prepared for your adventure.

Printed in Great Britain
by Amazon